Ways
to
SPARK
Your
Church
Program

Ways to SPARK Your Church Program

by

Frank A. Kostyu

ABINGDON PRESS
Nashville • New York

WAYS TO SPARK YOUR CHURCH PROGRAM
Copyright © 1974 by Abingdon Press

Library of Congress Cataloging in Publication Data

KOSTYU, FRANK A. Ways to spark your church program.
1. Pastoral theology. I. Title.
BV4011.K67   254'.6   73-12236

ISBN 0-687-44236-2

The photograph on page 104 was taken by Lynn Fitch.
All photographs, except those on pages 82 and 104,
were taken by Frank A. Kostyu and are the property
of *A.D.* magazine.

MANUFACTURED BY THE PARTHENON PRESS AT
NASHVILLE, TENNESSEE, UNITED STATES OF AMERICA

to
Frank and Julia Kostyu
my father and mother
who were Hungarian immigrants and
who
dedicated their lives
to the church

Preface

How many times has a church member turned in at his pastor's door and asked, "Do you have any ideas for our stewardship drive?" or "Do you have any new programs to suggest for evangelism?" The pastor may have anticipated such a question and prepared himself with a folder of suggestions. On the other hand, he is more than likely to respond with, "Well, I don't have anything to offer right now, but let me think about it." If he has been a "squirrel," he will turn to his files and see what he has on the subject. Too often he intended to save that idea, but . . . the cupboard is bare.

During the twenty years of my pastorate, I constantly sought program ideas and helps to carry on an effective ministry. Bulletins, newsletters, magazines, and newspapers provided ideas for improving our church program.

In pastoral circles there was an emphasis on the exchange of program helps. When a small group of ministers met on Friday mornings after dropping off our church announcements at the newspaper office, we would gather in the main street restaurant to share thoughts for church services, stewardship, missions and mission, evangelism, and similar concerns. Out of these discussions came some sparkling ideas.

When I continued my ministry through the written word as a magazine editor, one of my concerns was to zero in on those things related to the church and the pastor. I was on the alert for ideas that would assist the pastors, the lay men and women, the youth, and the church officers to spark their programs. I sought anything that would lead an individual involved in the life of a church to say, "Here is something we can try. Perhaps it will work for us as well."

This book is a storehouse of ideas for pastors and laymen alike. The minister can pass it along, saying, "Take a look at these suggestions. You will find some that we can develop in our program." Or an officer of the church will see a copy on the library shelf and find just what he has been searching for to get his particular program off the ground.

As you glance through this book, you will find a variety of useful suggestions. Some will fit your congregation as they are, others will have to be adapted to the situation, while still others will ignite similar ideas to help you carry on an effective ministry in your congregation.

Frank A. Kostyu
Montclair, New Jersey

Acknowledgments

In January 1971 the *United Church Herald* initiated a feature called "Leaders' Digest," which became a part of my responsibility for the magazine. The feature became an immediate success. Pastors, church leaders, and the man in the pew found in the columns ideas to spark local church programs. Ideas flowed to me from individuals throughout the country. Some of these submissions became a part of "Leaders' Digest" while others never made it because of lack of space. I have drawn on both the printed and the unpublished articles for this book.

I wish to thank the division of publication of the United Church Board for Homeland Ministries for permitting the copyrighted material and photographs that have appeared in the *United Church Herald* and the subsequent United Church Herald edition of *A.D.* to appear in this book. I am also grateful to the Reverend J. Martin Bailey, editor of *A.D.* and the former *United Church Herald,* for his help and cooperation in making this book possible. I want to thank each individual who sent his idea to our journal; I know that he will be pleased that his "spark" is helping other churches liven up their programs.

Rhoda Rhodes, librarian of *A.D.,* has been of invaluable help to me by calling many new church program innovations to my attention.

Another word of appreciation is due to my wife Marjorie for her valuable advice and nimble fingers as she typed the manuscript.

Contents

Aged

1. Sweetheart Calls

Once each year First Community Church in Columbus, Ohio, holds a series of home visits called the "Sweetheart Calls." Staff members call on ladies in the congregation who admit to being 65 years old or more. For each sweetheart there is a rose to brighten her day. Last year the staff visited more than 225 ladies. The program was begun by the late Roy Burkhart, psychiatrist and founding minister of the church. During May a sweetheart luncheon is held.

2. "Bedpad Brigade" Makes Articles for Aged and Others

Schwenkfelder Church in Palm, Pennsylvania, has two adult church school classes called "Helping Hands" and

13

"Willing Workers." For two years, the groups working together have been busy sewing bedpads for Phoebe Home for the Aged in Allentown, Pennsylvania.

Members gather in the church basement once a month to fold paper, cut plastic, patch, pin, and stitch material. Over five thousand bedpads have come off the Palm church assembly line since the groups began their project. Old sheets are solicited from individuals, laundry companies, hotels, and motels. After the pads are sewn, they are delivered by a member to the Phoebe Home.

If emergency programs arise, the brigade turns to other projects. In response to the Nicaraguan earthquake disaster, blankets were made and knotted from bolts of material donated by a nearby glove factory. Regular-size blankets are sent to the Pennsylvania Council of Churches to use with the migrant ministry program. Also, lap robes were recently prepared for Valley Forge Hospital.

Periodically, the colorful array of blankets is hung like banners in the morning worship service to show what has been accomplished.

A small group of women from the brigade meets weekly to quilt and keeps the community nurse supplied with welfare blankets.

When lunchtime comes, the women order "hoagies" from a nearby church organization which makes the sandwiches as their own fund-raising mission project.

3. Church Promotes Ten Commandments for the Aged

The pastor of Faith United Church of Christ in St. Joseph, Missouri, has offered his congregation and community a ten-point program of ministry to the aging.

1. Work to force nursing homes to meet minimum state requirements.
2. Sponsor "satellite" programs in other parts of the city for older church members and the local community.
3. Develop and operate Green Thumb, a program of ecology and a way of beautifying church property and neglected community property.
4. Develop a choir of the church's older adults to sing at worship services and to visit nursing homes and shut-ins.
5. Have periodic Sundays in which the church school is divided across age lines for interage communication.
6. Organize the aged for tours to visit mission projects, churches, and other places of interest.
7. Initiate a foster-grandparents' program to involve older adults whose families live in other communities.
8. Utilize the aged to work in day care centers.
9. Provide for the aged to be present at area youth events for witness and communication.
10. Honor the individuality and contributions of the aged to the church and community.

4. Program for Elderly

With a large public housing project to the west, an elderly population to the south, and a congregation with a high percentage of retired persons, Friedens Church in Milwaukee decided upon a mission to this age group.

A committee formed in the congregation designed a program called Eldercare. Within a few weeks the program was functioning and encountered a greater workload than had been anticipated.

The program started as a telephone service for the

elderly to call for transportation to a doctor or an occasional shopping trip. Eldercare then expanded so that it now provides transportation itself with a bus purchased by individual contributions and foundation grants. In addition, the members of Friedens volunteer time to drive or to provide other needed services to the aging or to the community.

One of the side effects of the program has been the assumption of leadership by the elderly themselves. Eldercare is coming under control and operation of the residents of the community as they answer the phones, schedule transportation, and determine policy on the board of directors.

5. Mission to the Aged

Part of the mission of Grand Avenue United Church of Christ, which is located in Milwaukee's inner city, is a series of free "Social Security" dinners for aged persons in the area. Other congregations cooperate with the members of Grand Avenue Church. The friendly fellowship is also important to lonely people.

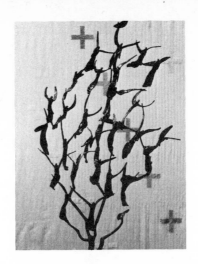

Art

6. Liturgical Macramé

The celebration task force of the Wellington Avenue Church in Chicago made use of a currently popular craft in its recent Easter plans. It commissioned a macramé (knot-tying) artist to design and make pulpit/lectern antependia, hangings for the front of an altar, lectern, or pulpit.

The hangings are multicolored and multitextured, combining macramé and weaving techniques. One section is purple, the liturgical color for Lent, and includes twisted yarn and knots of various sizes representing the agony and anguish of the betrayal and crucifixion. Another section is a small woven area of black, symbolic of the three days in the tomb. Finally, white yarn interwoven with brightly colored beads expresses the joy and hope of the resurrection and the promise of new life.

Banners are brightening sanctuaries everywhere. The

growing popularity of the ancient craft of macramé makes possible another medium through which lay people can express their faith not only during Easter but also throughout the year.

7. How to Use Pictures in Church Schools and Worship

Pictures can be found on walls and in sanctuaries and classrooms of our church schools, but not always with a maximum degree of effectiveness. A few practical suggestions may be helpful.

Pictures in church school

1. Pictures must be large enough and clear enough for all children to see them comfortably.
2. A picture is more effective if well-mounted on cardboard with a border one to three inches wide and of a tone to enhance the color values of the picture.
3. A picture should be displayed on a simple stand or easel at the eye level of the children.
4. Study of the picture may be stimulated by carefully preparing questions in advance by the class leader.
5. Allow plenty of time for the children to look, see, talk, and feel a picture's emotional impact.
6. With older children, use photographs of scenes, people, houses, artifacts. Put them on tackboards or bulletin boards for recall and repeated enjoyment. Do not leave them up forever!

Pictures in worship

1. Choose pictures carefully—only those that impart a worship mood.
2. Use a large picture, well-lighted. Use a spot if necessary.
3. Display picture against a good wall or curtain which has no distracting pattern or lines.

Pictures on walls
1. Hang pictures at eye level.
2. If framed in glass, avoid reflections.
3. Change pictures from time to time or on a regular basis to maintain freshness.

8. Simple Process for Sealing Pictures Used to Make Cross

The worship services of a Worthington, Ohio, church were enhanced by the addition of a new Celtic cross, hand-crafted by a member of the church. She chose the Celtic cross with its circle signifying eternity as most meaningful. On the circle she intertwined clasped hands of light skin tones and dark skin tones.

Pictures gathered by children and adults were carefully selected for placement behind a clear sheet of plexiglass. A solution called hyplar was applied between the plastic and the pictures and allowed to dry for a day. The paper backing was then washed away, leaving the images firmly attached to the plexiglass.

The use of hyplar would also be a way to do découpage, since it eliminates the thicknesses of paper.

The new Celtic cross (sometimes known as the Irish cross) was first used in a service of worship during the installation of the church's pastor.

9. Art Therapy

Art therapy has long been recognized by professionals in the field of mental health as a mode which "draws out" patients who otherwise might not be reached. Volunteers from the Church of the Savior in Knoxville, Tennessee, conduct art classes at the Eastern State Psychiatric Hospital. The response was so good that to relieve the crowded conditions, several groups had to be formed and a large auditorium used.

The paintings by the patients have been exhibited at the Church of the Savior, at the United Methodist Church, and at the University of Tennessee training center. Messiah Lutheran Church has also provided volunteers.

Various techniques have been used in the sessions: watercolors, crayons, acrylic materials, string art, collage, sketching, and printing.

10. Auction Proceeds Used for Art Program at Hospital

South Congregational Church in Peabody, Massachusetts, recently sponsored a project called Art and the Spirit. This was the seventh year for the event, which includes an auction.

More than one hundred paintings and other works of art were collected by a committee. On a Saturday in the dining room of the church, some three hundred persons gathered to participate in an auction. All the paintings and artifacts were sold and the proceeds, amounting to two thousand dollars, were presented to the volunteer arts and crafts program of the Danvers, Massachusetts, State Hospital.

Prior to the auction, guests had an opportunity to view some of the work by the hospital patients, whose craft materials and supplies were provided by previous auctions.

11. Happiness is a Hospital Scrapbook

Old magazines, newspaper clippings, snapshots, advertising, and greeting cards all go into the making of scrapbooks that can promote the thoughtfulness of the church toward the sick, the shut-ins, and the aged. Here are some guidelines:

1. Focus on the human interests and not on the sickness of your reader.
2. Make a scrapbook that is easy to handle.
3. Find positive, cheerful entries.
4. Do not degrade any race, religion, nationality, or occupation.
5. Use items that can be read in a few minutes.
6. Vary the entries on each page.
7. Allow margins of about two inches around the page.
8. Use mucilage, not tape.

12. Ten Notes on Successful Choir Festivals

A choir festival in your church can not only provide you with an afternoon of good church music but can also be a time of rich fellowship.

Here is an outline followed by a relatively small church:

1. Contact nearby choir directors by telephone and letter. Explain your interest in promoting a festival in which each choir might contribute one or two anthems.
2. Set up a tentative date, about five months in advance. A Sunday afternoon is appropriate.
3. Each participating choir sends to the host church the title and composer of its chosen music. In case of duplication, arrange for alternatives. Include in the program men, women, children, and youth who might want to sing contemporary music.
4. In a conference with all directors, choose three anthems to be sung by the combined choirs. Practice these

separately until the festival and then put it all together at a rehearsal prior to the festival.

5. Appoint a reception committee from the host church.
6. Borrow coat racks or arrange for coatroom space for choir robes.
7. Plan ahead. Mimeograph the seating plan for the choirs, location of office, restroom, and social hall.
8. Mimeographed programs should include order of the festival, names of ministers, organists, and churches taking part.
9. Arrange for the use of a tuned organ and piano.
10. Arrange for a coffee hour after the program.

13. Have a Hot-Topic Arts Festival

Try a sight-and-sound collage the next time you discuss a topic in your church. Cut pictures from newspapers and magazines and assemble a mural-montage. Tape your own background music and sounds.

Sing songs, serve food, play games, and make crafts that relate to the issues, people, and places you have chosen for your festival.

Church and Ministry

14. Celebrating a Church Anniversary

When a church is twenty-five years old, it customarily has a chicken or ham supper, charter members are given special recognition, and former clergymen are invited to participate. This usually takes one day.

Christ Church in Silver Spring, Maryland, took a year and a half to celebrate its birthday and did none of the above. Instead the church:

Held a community dialogue on urban problems;

Brought a German sociologist to "live in" with church members for a month;

Awarded $1,600 in prizes for a nationwide contest to create new church music;

Held a picnic and communion with a sister church;

Undertook an in-depth self study;

Raised twenty thousand dollars through "operation advance" to help finance the self study and to make needed repairs on the physical plant.

Motivating this form of celebration was the concept that a church should not look backward but should be a part of the community, celebrating its continuing life in that community.

15. Ninety-five Theses Reissued

The pastor of Immanuel Lutheran Church in Chicago wrote a new set of ninety-five theses for his congregation. After reading Luther's theses, he found many of them to be irrelevant to modern day customs and affairs. Something was needed to spark debate among the congregation and modern-day theologians. The contemporary theses grew out of discussion and dialogue with students, theologians, laymen, pastors, and his own personal pondering.

Some samples of the "new" theses are:

15. It is becoming progressively more impossible to be a Christian in a white, middle-class parish.

24. Unity is not only a beautiful idea, it is also Christ's plain command and our unconditional duty. The lack of unity will burn him like a fire.

33. The churches have been turning out a disheartened crowd of young folk, inoculated against any outbreak of creative religion.

43. The spirit of experimentation and creativity should dominate a church.

44. Your religion is useless to you until you have lost your proof texts, burned your sermon notes, and forgotten the

minutiae which you learned by heart for the examination.

50. People nowadays go to the church to be entertained and to the theater to be edified.

82. The poor in the church are the real treasure of the church.

87. All clergymen should have a second vocation. This would provide a chance to make a decent living and also to speak the truth without fear of economic reprisals from a parish.

16. Visuals Aid a Congregation's Life

How much of a congregation's life is visible on Sunday morning? Depending on a worship service to carry the message of the congregation may be asking too much of it. How can people be made aware of the richness of that congregation's life which goes unnoticed on Sunday morning?

The universal mimeograph has enabled every church to become its own publishing house—worship bulletins, newsletters, brochures. But more and more of people's time is spent in watching television. We need to become a film studio by having the needed materials in a tape recorder, a 35mm camera, and a slide projector. In this way the message of the church can go visually to prospective members, supplementing the printed material.

Here are a few concrete suggestions on how to create your own film studio. Take a piece of paper and divide it into three columns. In the first column keep a record of the numerical sequence of the slides. In the second column describe the picture which you want to photograph for that portion of the script. In the third column write the script.

Building a theme and the pictures to go with it is the hardest part of the assignment, but it is also the most exciting. After the paper work is the time to take those pictures. Turn loose those members of the congregation who are handy with a camera with an assignment describing the desired pictures. Then polish the script and tape it. This may take a few attempts before the audio part of the project has vitality and variety.

Put the slides into proper order, get the tape recorder ready, place the script before you, and advance the slides. This is the pay-off. There is a special chemistry when sound accompanies the slides!

What are the applications? One midwestern church reports that this tape-slide show has become the most effective tool they have to bring new people into their congregation. They take the projector and cassette recorder to the home of a prospective member and provide that family with an in-depth visual picture of their work and ministry. People have appreciated the presentation and have responded enthusiastically to it.

There are other applications, too. What annual congregational meeting doesn't need redemption? Show your people what they have been up to during the year, even if you must make a new slide show annually.

It is easy to edit the show to bring it up to date. Replace one slide with a current one, rewrite the script slightly, and there is a whole new show.

The mimeograph put you into the publishing business. That 35mm camera in your desk drawer may be the way to baptize the eyes of your viewers with the sparkle and brilliance of what God is doing with your congregation.

17. A Unique Pastorate

The Glenview Community Church in Mount Prospect, Illinois, has called a woman minister to perform a unique kind of ministry to the women of the church. The congregation numbers one thousand seven hundred members. The women's fellowship found a minister who was trained in counseling to help women with their own problems.

18. Kitchen Cabinet Evaluates Sunday Service

At Orchard Hill United Church of Christ in Chillicothe, Ohio, the minister announced, "By the narthex door is the sheet for you to sign up for the meeting of the Kitchen Cabinet today." He explains that both he and his deacons want feedback on the total service and on the sermon. The Kitchen Cabinet gives them such response.

Three adults and three young people go to the church kitchen after the service, have something to eat and drink, and frankly discuss their reactions to the order of the service and the sermon. A tape recorder records their discussion. On Monday the pastor listens to it. When the deacons meet, they, too, review the tape. Several suggestions have already been adopted.

The Kitchen Cabinet discussions are limited to forty-five minutes. Occasionally, however, they do run overtime. Since the pastor is not present, the comments tend to be open, frank, and uninhibited.

The ideas of the Kitchen Cabinet are appreciated, for dialogue from both youth and adults is helpful in closing the so-called generation gap. The sessions are another means of keeping the worship service and sermon "in tune" with the concerns and aspirations of the congregation, whose most significant witness is not in the gathered congregation but in the scattered congregation out in the world.

19. Getting to Know You

A minister arriving at a new pastorate in Nogales, Arizona, told about himself and his family visually. He gathered together a set of transparencies that depicted his life and that of his family. The slides followed him from his boyhood, through college and seminary, showing his marriage and the arrival of children. He put the picture together with music and text, using warm, personalized touches with all members of the family participating. Included in the presentation were imaginative hopes and dreams for the new ministry.

20. Nine Suggestions for Greeting New Church Staff Members

In the fall, many churches welcome new ministers, directors of Christian education, and other persons serving on the official church staff. In an article, "How to treat a new minister," the late Morgan P. Noyes of Montclair, New Jersey, offered the following ideas:
1. Remember that your new minister (or other leader) has been through a painful experience in leaving a church he loves. He or she may be homesick.
2. Tell him your name each time you see him for three months—he is meeting a lot of new people.
3. Give him information about sickness or trouble in church families.
4. If you cannot hear from where you sit, move to the front pews where you can.

5. Try to understand that your new minister can't call on every family first. He wants to visit your home as soon as he can.

6. Defend the freedom of the pulpit. Do not expect him to be entirely noncontroversial. Ask of him only that he be honest, thoughtful, courageous, with no loyalty above his allegiance to Christ.

7. Provide your minister with quiet time for reading and study.

8. Let him be himself, aware that no one expects him to be a replica of anybody else.

9. Look to him as your pastor, entitled to your cooperation, loyalty, prayers, and understanding.

21. Bump the Slump

What do you do about the summer slump in church attendance? Most parishes slump along with it. St. Martin's Episcopal Church, Ballwin, Missouri, had the sense to ask why it had a slump and to discuss it. One lay person said the parish needed more services, not less. The Missourians found that by assuming attendance will be low, and therefore that one service is enough, some people are discouraged from coming. "We decided there was no way the congregation could be split worse than it already was by the one service: 10 percent in the church and 90 percent somewhere else . . . so we went to four services a week." They chose one midweek program for those out of town on weekends, one on Saturday night ("Roman Catholics seem to like that. Maybe Episcopalians will, too"), an early one Sunday for those who want the rest of the day free, and a

Sunday service at the conventional hour. Results: attendance up 100 percent and treasury operational, too.

22. Five Marks of a Successful Church

One: A precise indicator of a church's success is how much of its money it gives away. Churches are in business to lose money. A church's profit is its loss. Jesus lost everything. "Whoever loses his life for my sake will find it." That is how Christians are made.

Two: A precise indicator of a church's success is how many of its people it gives away. "I was sick and you visited me." It is a matter of giving more than money, a matter of giving self. "I was in prison and you came to me."

Three: A third measure of a church's success is how attractive it is to young people. Mark was a boy at the end of Jesus' life. Barnabas was his cousin. Timothy was a young man. Onesimus, the slave, was young. Paul was young: "They laid their garments at the feet of a young man named Saul." Jesus himself was relatively young.

Four: A fourth measure of a church's success is how controversial it is in its community. The whole thing began in controversy. Jesus was executed as an insurrectionist. He taught in controversy. He died in controversy. The precise charge against him was "He stirs up the people."

The church has always had an uneasy relation with the culture in which it exists. It is a radical group, following a radical leader, and it will do radical things. If it does not, then it is not the church.

Five: The final measure of a successful church is how honest it is about style. Jesus was. He knew what he had to do. That's content. He also knew how to do it. That's style. He knew how he had to do it. No one else had put the Messiah and the Suffering Servant together. He did. This is perhaps the most brilliant example of style in history. And when his own friend, Peter, threatened to get in the way of his style, Jesus called him "Satan" to his face. Jesus' style was suffering. So was the early church's.

23. Nine Steps for Clustering Congregations

"Cluster ministries" is suggested as an appropriate way to strengthen each local church. In a cluster arrangement, congregations within a limited geographical area work together in a variety of ways and in differing organizational patterns.

Clusters are making it possible for congregations to move from competitive to cooperative relationships, for clergy to discover new collegiality, and for declining churches to find new options for the future.

In a booklet, "Clusters," the Rev. Theodore H. Erickson of the United Church Board for Homeland Ministries and the Rev. Robert Macfarlane of the United Presbyterian Church suggest the following guidelines for the development of church clusters:

1. The participation of both clergy and lay leaders is critical to the development of a cluster.
2. Spend enough time (up to eighteen months) identifying the specific "mission" of the cluster in the community.
3. Clear, short-term goals should be stated together with suggested strategies for implementation.
4. Goals, expectations, and motivations need to be reevaluated from time to time.
5. Allow time and make opportunities for trust relation-

ships based on interpersonal understandings as well as on common agreements on tasks to be undertaken.

6. Keep your association or conference informed and study the *Guide for Interchurch Action* developed by the Consultation on Church Union.

7. Provide for full communication within participating congregations.

8. Develop realistic budgets.

9. Be patient.

24. How to Manage Conflict in Your Church

At times a credibility gap develops between church leadership and the congregation. When this occurs, leaders and laity may find it hard to communicate. Narrow-mindedness on controversial issues can be the result.

While some diversity of opinion is to be expected and is good for the church, lack of creativity in dealing with conflict can hinder its growth.

In view of these problems, here are some suggestions:

1. Hold open congregational meetings to discuss controversial topics. Allow plenty of time before the meetings to obtain as much relevant information as possible from national agencies, conferences, and associations; then circulate it among the church members.

2. Check on the accuracy of potentially controversial statements made by other levels of the church. Realize that the press sometimes distorts information, so do not assume the reports are correct. Verify the facts.

3. Using Bible passages, audio-visual materials, and other resources, discuss at a congregational meeting the need for and the definition of Christian social responsibility.

4. Develop questionnaires for the congregation to ascertain their viewpoints with respect to areas of conflict.
5. Know how your delegates to meetings will vote on these issues; make sure they represent the general opinions of the congregation.

25. Prayer and Sharing

Immanuel Church in Dalton, Illinois, has several prayer and sharing groups for the purpose of growing in effective and powerful use of prayer for others, self, the church, and the world. The groups are kept small—six to eight people. Out of the weekly meetings has come a sharing of trust among those present. An openness has developed with respect to needs, concerns, and experiences. The group should, if possible, include both sexes and a variety of ages.

26. Some Changes Made

At Rockford, Illinois, the Spring Creek Congregational Church was frustrated with the sameness of their worship services. They organized a small task force to study the situation. The group had two purposes in mind—to plan celebration worship services and to work with twelve other churches in the area to sponsor a celebration workshop. For this, they sought the leadership of the Center for Contemporary Celebration in Chicago. The most commendable part of the project is that it was initiated, with the approval of the ministers, by lay people.

27. Dialogue Brings Healthy Response

Union Church in Moline, Illinois, has found that lay participation in services has brought a new interest and resurgence in worship. They use a worship aid bulletin insert called "This Week" on which is printed various contemporary liturgical aids—responsive prayers, music, Scripture, and readings. These forms are varied with discussion in worship. One Sunday the minister and a layman spoke on the topic of faith and daily work. On another Sunday a dialogue took place regarding illness and death. The response to such services has been so positive that discussions have had to be terminated because of time limits, even though the congregation expressed an eagerness to continue.

28. Five-Phase Fellowship

"Putting it all together" is the theme that the First Church of Christ in West Hartford, Connecticut, gave their new unstructured program on Sunday mornings. Five divisions followed a 10 to 11 A.M. worship service: studies in faith was an exploration of relevant topics—miracles, prayer, family life, death, drugs, and others—led by competent leaders; exploring the sermon included a time of debate and sharing; small groups led by laymen discussed the sermon. The hour is regarded as a means to communicate with the minister, with coffee served to lubricate the vocal cords. The topic "Are You There?" deals with the complex social and political issues of the day. Abortion, problems of the aged, prison reform, welfare, and campus ministries are other areas which are considered. The children's hour includes fifty craft projects under the supervision of professional leaders. For those not wishing to be involved in group discussion or activity, the coffee and conversation provide a time of meeting friends.

29. Threefold Anniversary

When Emanuel Church in Irvington, New Jersey, celebrated their seventy-fifth anniversary, they had a threefold celebration—worship to God, fellowship with one another, and outreach to the community. The fellowship of one to another included an invitation to nine community organizations to display their programs and projects in the church fellowship hall. Among those participating were the day-care council, hospital, police athletic league, lapidary society, garden club, art associates, historical society, development corporation, and mineralogist society. This opened up new relationships with organizations in the city. Emanuel found it a good way to learn more about opportunities in a community.

30. Friendliness in the Pew

Here are five simple steps to a friendlier church: 1. Speak to the other person first. Do not wait for someone else to take the initiative. 2. If you do not know the persons around you, introduce yourself. 3. Wear a pleasant expression. If you have to be grumpy or sour, act this way someplace else. Keep in mind that Christianity is a religion of joy. 4. Make the testimony of Will Rogers your own, "I never met a person I did not like." 5. Memorize and practice Proverbs 18:24, "There are friends who pretend to be friends, but there *is* a friend who sticks closer than a brother."

31. Show and Tell in Church

The Good Samaritan Church in Pinellas Park, Florida, has what they call a time of sharing during the worship

35

hour. At a designated moment during the service, the members are free to report on things past, announce things to come, or comment about striking experiences in their lives. Visiting friends are introduced, local political issues are sometimes brought out, and the good news of engagements, marriages, birth of children, and recovery of the sick is shared. The joys and sorrows belong to all. The happy freedom of such sharing has brought the congregation closer together.

32. The First Breakfast

The members of the United Church of Gainesville, Florida, went fishing in the Atlantic surf. Some members baked their favorite breads. Then on Sunday morning the congregation met for worship in celebration, not of the Last Supper, but of the First Breakfast. The elements were biblical bread and fish, partaken of on tables set in the form of a square. Part of the service included hymn singing, the singing of Malotte's "The Lord's Prayer," guitar music, silent meditation, an anthem by the choir, and a time of sharing. The minister preached on the meaning of bread and fish, two foods described in the New Testament. "When they had finished breakfast . . . ," a hymn was sung, there was a moment of silence, and then fellow worshipers greeted each other.

33. Yeast and Leaven

Unbaked loaves of bread were carried by canvassers of First Church of Christ in Sharon, Connecticut, to those they visited on stewardship Sunday. The bread was rising, and the families were asked to bake it during the visits. The minister said, "It made it easier for all to see the mission of the church, the coming of the kingdom, as the leaven, the yeast in the world."

34. Straight in the Eye

At the Southern Hills United Church in Boulder, Colorado, the congregation took out the pews in the sanctuary and brought in chairs. These were arranged in a circle. Now the congregation faces one another across the crowded room. As one worshiper remarked, "It means that I am not looking at the back of someone's head. The circle with the worship center in the middle makes a difference."

35. Art in Listening

At Faith Church in St. Joseph, Missouri, the minister was concerned about the children in the congregation who appeared inattentive during the sermon. Instead of asking them to go to their own service in another part of the building, he inaugurated sermon helpers. Prior to the sermon, the minister listed six things the children should look for in his sermon. They were then to draw their impressions of each. The pictures were then displayed in the vestibule until the following Sunday when a new group was put up.

Church Seven Days a Week

36. Church Houses Kidney Center

A little-used church school room was put to a new service when the Lombard Community Kidney Center was dedicated in First Church, Lombard, Illinois.

The medical director of the house staff of West Suburban Hospital in Oak Park, an authority on kidney diseases, was the director. He was also responsible for the supervision and coordination of the project that houses two kidney dialysis machines, which he and the Illinois Department of Health cooperatively provide.

Since patients sometimes remain in the center for six to eight hours, a lounge area, a pullman kitchen, two hospital beds, and a color TV are made available.

"Patients are selected entirely by the doctors to whom we rent the facilities for one dollar a year," said the pastor of First Church. "We are pleased to provide this center for the healing of the body, which is tied to the healing of the soul."

A spokesman for the Kidney Foundation of Illinois estimates that more than 3,700 people in the United States are using this kind of machine. In Illinois about 320 people need the dialysis equipment and approximately twice that number die each year from lack of the treatment it provides.

37. Summer Program Leads to Family Happenings

Every Tuesday night this past summer at the Sherman Congregational Church in Connecticut, a group of talented parents, aware of the teen-age "there's nothing to do" syndrome, created the "Tuesday Happening."

Between 7:30 and 10 P.M. a dozen adults and sometimes almost three times as many young people from the eighth grade through high school met in the church parish hall to learn arts and crafts and games.

The "happening" was sponsored by the church's Christian education committee. One adult taught clay modeling while her husband, an architect, was in charge of the water-color enthusiasts. Another architect taught the art of macramé—knot-tying—to create anything from vests and bags to artistic wall hangings.

Other people taught creative writing, block printing, weaving, and creative stitchery. For a change of pace for those less artistically inclined, there were game tables. Adults taught chess and bridge.

The church group also sponsored teen-age summer dances.

38. Church Organizes Counseling Clinic with Retired Members

Pass-a-Grille Beach Community Church in St. Petersburg, Florida, has opened a counseling clinic in the church. A talent sheet circulated among the members revealed that there were retired, professionally trained members in the congregation, so the idea of a counseling clinic was born. The women's fellowship of the church sponsored the project.

The clinic is open every Wednesday afternoon from 1 to 4 P.M. The counselees are greeted by a receptionist in the church library, take light refreshments, and then have a private consultation with a trained counselor. Every effort is made to resolve a person's problem; sometimes several visits, telephone calls, and advice from lawyers or other professionals are required.

Taking advantage of the confidential help program are high school and college students, middle-aged couples with marital problems, drug users, potential suicides, alcoholics, individuals with sex problems, and young couples seeking premarital advice.

Expenses are kept to a minimum. Since the staff is made up of volunteers, there are no salaries to pay. Space in the church is provided by the congregation, and office supplies are paid for by the women's fellowship. Small gifts to the clinic have been used to help those who need immediate financial assistance until their cases can be channeled to available agencies.

39. Kansas City Church Opens Its Doors for Weekday Program

Many churches stand vacant from one Sunday to another while community organizations go without meeting space. This is not true at Country Club Church in Kansas City, Missouri, which is open for business seven days a week.

The church's numerous rooms are used for community activities. The church sponsors troops for Boy and Girl Scouts, Brownies, and Senior Scouts. Six parent-teen school groups from Southwest High School meet at the church on a regular basis.

The church also operates a registered preschool and provides facilities for the Happy Hut Teen Town, a social activity for handicapped children.

A Roman Catholic catechism class meets regularly in one of its rooms, and a number of nonprofit organizations like the Heart of America Soccer Association, the Heart of America Nu Voice Club, and the Southwest Area Educational Council also use the church's facilities.

In addition, Country Club Church sponsors the meal-a-month project in Kansas City. Through this plan, each member of the congregation is asked to bring a meal each month to the church. This is then taken to a needy family.

To provide clothing for those in need, the Jackson County Clothes Closet was established at the church.

"When we considered how much unused space we had available," said the pastor, "we were glad to make it available for our community. Any church, large or small, can do the same. It does my heart good to see people coming in and going out of our building all week. There is life here!"

41

Ecumenism

40. Churches Pool Resources for Christian Education

In the town of Vermillion, South Dakota, four churches—First Baptist, the United Methodist, St. Paul's Episcopal, and the United Church of Christ—have undertaken a new cooperative program of Christian education. There are 160 children enrolled in the church school from kindergarten through sixth grade. Classes are conducted by eighteen teachers for an hour and fifteen minutes each week, and an average of 93 percent of the enrollment attends.

How did this project come about? A committee was formed to determine the needs of the churches. It decided that competition among the churches was a luxury they could no longer afford.

The director of the school, Elizabeth Cutting, said, "People are interested in Christian education, but with the present mobility, families go away for weekends. So our classes are held during the week. The public school released the children for religious instruction, and our attendance has increased two and a half times since we began."

To promote professional standards the teachers are given a small honorarium, and the director's salary is borne by the cooperating churches according to the number of children they send to the program. The school is incorporated so that it can buy property and a bus.

Three youth groups which meet for various projects throughout the week have grown out of the school. During school vacation the groups traveled to California. They also went to Washington, D.C. and New York City to participate in a political seminar and a youth discussion at the UN.

41. Glad Days

Five churches in Nashua, New Hampshire—Arlington United Methodist, Church of the Resurrection, Pilgrim, First United Church of Christ and St. Christopher's Catholic Church—held a "Glad Days" summer school. Sessions were provided for preschoolers and grades one through six in the public schools.

Themes were "Creating a New World," "Experiencing a Breakthrough," "Finding God in Our Backyards," "Hope in the Future," and "Celebration of Joy and Hope." Glad Day activities included releasing balloons, singing, hikes, faith walks, small group sessions, team teaching, guitars, celebrating, and loving. Ministers and priests shared in the group celebrations.

42. An Ecumenical Confirmation Program
for the Small Community

One of the chief concerns of denominations and pastors is to provide adequate confirmation and church membership training for young people. To carry on such a program is particularly difficult in a small town where churches have limited resources and frequently compete with each other.

Four churches—two Methodist churches, a United Church of Christ, and an Episcopal church—in Lisbon, New Hampshire, a small town just north of the White Mountains, solved the problem by uniting for a two-year preconfirmation instruction period for their seventh and eighth graders. The class meets on Monday afternoons.

The United Church of Christ pastor (who also serves the two United Methodist churches) shares teaching duties along with the Episcopalian rector. When the young people reach the ninth grade, each pastor takes his own group for the final year of instruction.

The first year of the ecumenical class focuses on the Bible, tracing the growth of the concept of God from the polytheism of the patriarchs to the concepts of Paul and the early church.

A secondary theme traces the actual writing of the Bible from the earliest oral tradition to today's modern translations. The second year starts with the church as described in Acts and ends with the discussion of COCU (Consultation on Church Union).

43. Community Seminar on Death and Dying Lessens Fears

Does a congregation have a ministry to perform in the crisis of death—something more than saying a few words over the remains? What can be done to prepare people for death? How can the patient and his family better cope with a terminal illness?

These were some questions that led the pastor of First Congregational Church in New London, Wisconsin, to develop a community service program. The seminars used various resource persons including physicians, funeral directors, a chaplain, a lawyer, an investment broker, and an insurance agent.

The first evening was spent discussing the stages of terminal illnesses and the normal grief process. A program on the medical profession's dilemmas about prolonging life or prolonging dying and placing the responsibility for turning off the machines followed.

The third seminar addressed itself to the funeral business. Included was not only the historical background of funerals but also a discussion of costs and the value of preplanning.

The fourth seminar centered around alternatives to the funeral business such as memorial societies and willing the body (or certain vital organs) for medical study.

The last meeting of the series dealt with death and the legal implications, including estate planning.

Each session was scheduled for one and a half hours, divided into formal presentation by resource persons, followed by a discussion and a question and answer period. Some of those persent were staff persons from the hospital and from two senior citizens' homes. Many have since indicated how helpful the meetings proved to be in deepening their relationships with their patients.

Several unexpected but happy by-products included: the pastor's being invited to relate to the family much earlier in the terminal illness process; a serious evaluation of the congregation's and the pastor's ministries at the time of death; a greater freedom of the family to choose the funeral most meaningful for them.

44. A New Twist to Christmas

On the Sunday before Christmas the members of various churches in Watertown, Connecticut, have eliminated pageants, vespers, and church programs in favor of a new form of celebration. At 6:00 P.M. members of the churches gather at Christ Episcopal Church to sing a few carols and hear the scriptural account of the Christmas story. The entire congregation then walks to the steps of Trinity Lutheran Chapel where more carols are sung and prayers offered.

A walk of five hundred feet brings the group into the sanctuary of First Congregational Church. There, in candlelight, the worshipers listen to the handbell choir share Christmas selections. The procession moves to the United Methodist Church to continue the celebration with more singing and music by the young people of the church. The final portion of the walk is down the main street to St. John's Roman Catholic Church for the singing of "Joy to the World" and participation in refreshments.

Those who are unable to walk in the procession are transported by car to each church.

The purpose of the service is to celebrate as a community and to nurture the ecumenical spirit in the churches.

45. From Small Beginnings

The United Methodist, Missouri Lutheran, Southern Baptist, Roman Catholic, and United Church of Christ churches in Frankfort, Illinois, have been doing things together for four years. It began on a Labor Day Sunday with a worship service. Another service was held in Lent. A Christian United Committee was formed which developed an interchurch program for ten softball teams made up of young people of all denominations playing on each team. Every month the clergy meet to discuss community problems or some theological issue.

46. Canvass at the Mall

Anglican, United Church, and Catholic women in Rossland, British Columbia, organized an ecumenical team of thirty-eight teen-agers to canvass shoppers in a local mall to raise funds for Pakistani refugees. They collected $338 in one day.

Education

47. Television Used as Information Tool

A church in Ithica, New York, found a new approach to the problem of trying to involve parents in the work of their children in the church school. Many parents teach, but others have little tangible contact with what is actually being accomplished in classes. Even those who teach often do not realize what is happening at other grade levels.

Through the cooperation of several laymen in the church, four classes were video taped in action on a Sunday morning. One week later a documentary was presented to parents who came to a family dinner. Segments of the tape were combined with live sound from each class.

For the showing, the parents sat around monitor sets. After each class was shown, time was allowed for questions and discussion. The pastor, teachers, board of Christian education members, and resource leaders were all involved.

48. The "Difference" Is Beauty

Vacation church school at Mayflower Congregational Church in Minneapolis used the theme "Differences Are Beautiful."

The ninety enrolled children visited the Afro-American Culture Center at Fifth Avenue Congregational Church, took a trip to the Indian Museum and Trading Post at Mille Lacs, and studied Jewish festival occasions, eating Jewish food.

Literature was developed for parents to use in supplementary home activities, providing information about other races and culture.

The school concluded with a Sunday service at which the pastor of St. Peter's African Methodist Episcopal Church was preacher.

49. A Sunday School with a Difference

One fall Sunday the Southern Hills Church in Boulder, Colorado, opened its windows, and the traditional church school concept blew right out into the mountains. What remained did not look like a Sunday school. All ages from the first grade (in public school) through adults were thrown together across the age span. There were no divisions according to age.

The theme of the first session was "Journey into Time," which was approached from three different aspects—puppets, music, and history.

A following theme was the "Times of Jesus," also approached via puppets, music, and historical meaning.

The objectives of the format were threefold:

1. Bring families together to aid communication with one another while pursuing a common Christian education theme.

2. Develop a dialogue between persons of all ages which in turn would help people to better understand both themselves and others.

3. Provide a form which allows flexibility in learning. Special workshops zeroed in on Advent craft and the celebration of the Jewish festival of Hanukkah.

50. Ten Steps to Better Reading

Help each member of your congregation to discover new pleasures and a wider world with ten steps to better reading. An informed membership can help spark a church program. Pass along these personalized steps:

1. Set aside some time each day for uninterrupted reading.
2. Select a place to read that is comfortable and quiet.
3. Plan for variety in the subjects about which you want to read.
4. Decide to read at least three books on the same general subject during a three-month period.
5. Do not limit yourself to a single subject or writing style. From time to time break up the reading with a novel, mystery, or mind-stretching article.
6. Keep a list of the books and major articles you read.
7. If the book belongs to you, underline significant passages.

8. Read one dependable news magazine or newspaper to inform yourself about the world in which you live.
9. Using the Bible as a guide, check your reactions to current events in the light of its teachings.
10. Discuss what affects you in your daily life with another person or with a group in your church. Your perceptions will be sharpened by those who differ with you.

51. How to Use Your Denominational Publication

1. Review and discuss selected articles in board and committee meetings.
2. Encourage church school teachers to supplement the curriculum.
3. Use articles in your church magazine as discussion starters in group meetings.
4. The suggested meditations and materials can be used in sermons and speeches.
5. References to articles, features, and news can be used in sermons and speeches.
6. Make posters from the art work by cutting pictures and quotations from your magazine. Work out original designs. Post on the bulletin boards.
7. Sponsor essay contests with topics dealt with in your journal—Christmas art, race stewardship, poverty, age, denominational events, and personal problems.
8. Use your magazine in youth meetings for discussion.
9. Place a copy of your magazine in the local public library.
10. Use the magazine to acquaint new members with the programs of the denomination.
11. Ask a competent person to present a digest of the

important stories at a church meeting. Note particularly new ideas in the articles.

52. Elective Courses

Villa Park (Illinois) Community Church has a new church program that permits each person in the church school to select a variety of courses, every one being developed over a ten-week period. Three themes are designated—studies of Christianity, social and world involvement, creative expression. The program involves more teachers over a shorter period of time than the traditional form and includes teacher training during September. Classes begin in October.

53. Start-Stop Method Finds Success in Education Courses

The Frankford Congregational Church in Philadelphia has been successful with a start-stop approach to adult Christian education. The idea is to plan for a series of short-term studies on various topics, each with an announced terminal date. The period between classes is utilized for reflection on the course just finished and planning for the upcoming one.

Evaluating material for study might be one phase of the curriculum—a book, a series of articles in a magazine, or a number of topics relating to a subject of current interest.

54. Confirmation Instruction Utilizes New Approach

The ninth grade can be a crucial year for young people —a year to examine values for themselves beyond those of their peers, to explore the ultimate purposes for living and the kind of life-style one can build.

Confirmation education might at first sound a bit foreign to all of this, but it's not. In this legendary age of Aquarius, ninth grade might well be the year of reaffirmation for those preparing for full, responsible membership in the Christian community.

Instruction for confirmation has taken on a new approach at Christ Church in Bethlehem, Pennsylvania. At the beginning of the program, a parent orientation session was held to acquaint the family with the mode of instruction and the goals of the instruction period. There were three basic units.

Unit one was conducted on Sunday morning during the Sunday church school hour with lay teachers instructing the entire class for thirteen Sundays.

Unit two was a weekend fellowship retreat held at a nearby conference center, helping to develop fellowship and community among the participants.

Unit three included instruction in the fundamentals of Christian faith and tradition by the three pastors of the church. Each one taught for two twelve-week periods in a designated area. Then the class rotated to another pastor.

55. Alternative Christian Education

The formation of a task force on alternative Christian education has evinced a genuine concern for quality Christian learning at Glenview Community Church in Mount Prospect, Illinois. Members have shown openness and honesty by challenging one another while still maintaining respect for the ideas of other individuals.

The task force has developed alternative Sunday school concepts to expand Christian education yet not replace the traditional. The church school now has family clusters where there is a recognition that the family is basically responsible for a child's Christian education. The parents learn with their children.

Another concept is retreat education, a mini-family camp, to allow for concentration on value-building. In addition, weekday experiences evolved after the question, "Who says Sunday school has to meet only on Sunday or on Sunday at all?" was discussed.

56. Sunday School Meets on Wednesdays

Grades four, five, and six of the Falmouth United Church of Christ in Falmouth, Maine, meet on Wednesday instead of Sunday. (The Roman Catholic Church and Fireside Community Church also have religious instruction on Wednesday.) Total attendance, as well as average attendance, has almost doubled. Because Wednesday classes follow public school classes, absenteeism is low and teacher recruitment is easier.

At the request of the Falmouth public school officials, parents sign permission slips authorizing school bus drivers to drop children at their church after school. Parents are then responsible for picking up their children at the end of the church school session.

The Wednesday classes provide opportunity to use most of the church facilities. When a class project requires elbow room, extra space is easily provided. Additional resource people are more readily available, and the pastor has a better chance to be with the children than if the classes were held on Sunday.

One disadvantage of the Wednesday classes is that parents of children who do not attend Falmouth public schools have to drive them both directions. A few families attend church less frequently.

Preclass activities include punch and cookies, music, and organized games.

57. Midhour Program Supplements Christian Education Needs

Over nine months ago the board of Christian education of Plymouth Congregational United Church of Christ in Des Moines, Iowa, began researching ways to meet the church's educational needs. The board's task force decided that the "midhour" was for them. A new program has been adopted that offers:

1) Six-week courses to all age groups on Bible study, theology, and ethical issues.

2) An interest group for creative dance, banner-making, simulation games, arts and crafts, and media workshops.

3) Courses and activities led by specialists in psychology, law, prison reform, campus ministry, social work, art, and journalism.

4) The church schedule from January to June is:
First service and church school 9:00-10:00
Midhour 10:10-10:50
Second service 11:00-12:00

The congregation has been asked to suggest learning ideas and further study programs. Periodic evaluations will be made.

58. Five Questions to Help You Evaluate Education in Your Church

1. How has your educational program been shaped to the needs of your people and your mission?
2. Are you using new resources to enrich, supplement, and update your program?
3. Are your youth involved in the decision-making processes? Is your youth program *by* rather than *for* youth?
4. When did your educational leaders last observe the innovative methods being used in your hometown public school classrooms?
5. Do you offer weekday or summer activities as alternatives to faltering Sunday programs?

Environment

59. California Church Promotes
Ecology Education Programs

The San Ramon Valley Church in Danville, California, has made environmental protection a primary concern of its church program.

The congregation is involved in ecology in at least three ways: a monthly full-page article on ecology appears in their newsletter; a five-day youth camp on ecology was held last summer, and a four-week worship/education series has been held.

The newsletter article is submitted by a member of the church who has moved from the community but who still keeps contact with her friends. She covers topics like phosphates in detergents, support for a park dedication ordinance, encouragement of the use of bicycles, and the establishment of bike paths in Danville.

The ecology camp involved thirty-five high-school-age youth. They lived, worked, and studied in the church for five days. Together they cleaned junk from a road to Mount Diablo and made a sculpture from it. Then, putting it on the back of a truck, they paraded through town displaying it. The young people also became involved in other ecology projects, finishing off their week together by leading the Sunday morning worship service.

The most involved effort was the worship-education series on ecology. The congregation worshiped together for forty-five minutes and then met for the same length of time for an education period.

During the five weeks of this series the pastor tried some spectacular demonstrations during the worship—one Sunday morning he threw a dirty soda can on the chancel floor, where he had already collected a pile of garbage, to show how people defame sacred places.

60. Churches Emphasize Environmental Stewardship

Many churches are getting down to earth—at least in their efforts to protect the environment. In Santa Barbara, California, First Congregational United Church of Christ sponsored an ecology tour to show members the effects of waste in their own neighborhoods. In Des Moines, Iowa, members of Plymouth Congregational United Church of Christ spearheaded a community-wide drive that salvaged a trainload of paper. Church school classes at Watchung Congregational United Church of Christ in Montclair, New Jersey, delittered the streets, and one member fenced off an area of the church lawn to show how much grass is required to return enough oxygen to the air for one person. But remember, the stewardship of our natural resources needs to be a continuing concern of the churches, rather than a one-time effort.

61. A Box Program Dramatizes the Environment of Man

Two high school boys designed and painted a maze of cardboard boxes to illustrate concepts about living and environment at the United Methodist Church in Ridgewood, New Jersey, on Stewardship Sunday. Written and pasted on the sides of the boxes were words and pictures about the rich, the poor, and the uses of money. People attending the program went through the maze. As they emerged, they were confronted by young people wearing masks and mimicking stereotypes of the rich and the poor.

Those attending the program then went through a cafeteria line and received their dinners in cardboard boxes. They were seated at tables decorated with boxes and placemats on which were written phrases such as "Jesus was responsible" or "care enough." In the dinner boxes were crayons and instructions on how each person could decorate his own box.

At the end of the dinner, two actors presented *The Box* by Eve McFall, and the film *Pursuit of Happiness: the Materialistic Way* was shown. During the movie young people, decorated with boxes, circulated about the room chanting words and phrases about the complexities of an affluent culture.

A second film, *Hunger in America* (a CBS documentary), was projected on one half of a very large screen (several sheets sewn together) , while on the other half the chairman of the stewardship committee used an overhead projector to show the church budget. The contrast pointed out the enormous needs of society and the small amount of funds given to the world by the local church.

After the film ended, the side walls of the auditorium were bathed with projections of slides of persons in Ridgewood, aerial views of the city, pictures of the church and its work—a bombardment of sensory experiences climaxing the presentations by bringing the message home.

Evangelism

62. Suggestions for Revitalizing a Church

How do you breathe life into a dead organization? The pastor of First Baptist Church in Hollywood, Florida, where membership in five years has increased from five hundred to two thousand, follows four steps:

1. He offers the people a deep spiritual direction.
2. He creates an organization that functions.
3. He shows deep love for all people.
4. He is enthusiastic.

To revive the church, he also:

1. Helped develop *esprit de corps* among members.
2. Organized the church school, emphasizing the biblical content of the curriculum.
3. Instituted a visitation program.
4. Cleaned up the properties by trimming the lawns, painting the building, and washing the walls.

5. Began an advertising campaign, using radio, newspapers, signboards, and bus stop ads. Circulars were sent home with church school children.
6. Created a vision for the future. This included expansion in numbers, an increase in baptisms, and financial growth.
7. Built a youth program because "young people reflect vitality in a church."

63. Five Questions to Help You Evaluate Outreach in Your Church

1. Do you have a well-balanced inreach-outreach program?
2. Have any of your members visited mission projects in the U.S. or overseas?
3. Does your church accept the principle of diversity and variety in its outreach activity?
4. Do you ask, "Can we involve other churches in our community concerns?"
5. Is the concept of regional community planning understood and accepted by your members and your church leaders?

64. Five Ideas to Help You Improve Your Outreach

1. Adopt an "open building" policy for community events.
2. Set up a "help line" for your area with a twenty-four-hour ministry.
3. Use "image explosions" as moments of concern. Example: Five children go to chancel steps and shiver. Three others come forward with blankets. Two continue to shiver. The needs of Church World Service are graphically demonstrated.

4. Organize a tutorial center with the cooperation of schools and parents.
5. Set up a "missions mart" with handcrafts purchased and sold as a self-help project.

65. Five Questions to Help You Evaluate Fellowship in Your Church

1. To what extent do members of your church know and care about one another?
2. How does your congregation help its members to serve one another's personal needs?
3. What efforts are made to draw visitors, fringe participants, and new members into the life of the church?
4. What opportunities do you provide for adequate sharing of concerns, interests, hopes, etc., among the members of the congregation?
5. To what extent do fellowship activities genuinely meet the personal needs of members as well as the organizational needs of the congregation?

66. Five Ideas to Help You Improve Your Fellowship Program

1. Use part of each committee or board meeting to share concerns which participants bring from their lives.
2. When you have more than twelve persons, encourage full participation by first sharing in groups of two or three.
3. To encourage meaningful sharing, pose nonthreatening questions which elicit responses revealing feelings and values as well as facts.
4. Hold meetings designed to deepen fellowship in informal, relaxed settings (in living rooms or in a circle).

5. Experiment with longer blocks of time (morning and afternoon; afternoon and evening; weekend). Try this instead of shorter, regularly scheduled meetings.

67. Parable of the New Neighbor

A certain man moved into our community. He didn't fall among thieves, he just moved in. By chance a neighbor came by and saw him. The neighbor said, "I'm running late in my schedule today and besides, the preacher probably knows about him."

In like manner another neighbor came to that place, and passing by on the other side, said, "I don't believe in being a fanatic about religion. I'll wait until he brings up the subject of the church; then I'll invite him to our church if he has time."

But a certain neighbor as he journeyed came where he was, and when he saw him he was moved with compassion and stopped by to welcome him into the church the next Lord's Day. He even offered to come by for him, which he did. On Sunday morning he turned him over to the Sunday school superintendent and said, "Take care of this man for me and whatever else I can do, I'll do it."

Now which of these do you think was a neighbor unto him who moved into our community? Go and do thou likewise.

68. Meet the People

"Project: Getting To Know You" was a smash hit at Sacred Heart Parish in Eureka, California, and is being adopted by other congregations. Getting to know the people of a big parish or congregation is a problem. Laymen came up with this suggestion:

The pastor invited ten couples to supper at the rectory on a Sunday evening. The following Sunday, ten more couples were invited—but the guests of the previous week returned to prepare the food and act as hosts. Thus the round-robin began.

A typical Sunday night at the rectory: both groups (guests and hosts) meet at the church for a service at 5:15 P.M. Following the service, the hosts become chefs in the kitchen while the guests get acquainted and chat with the pastor. Couples are chosen alphabetically from the parish rolls and thus a cross-section of parishioners is present every Sunday.

69. Church on Wheels

The Catawba County Fair in Hickory, North Carolina, had a surprisingly popular sideshow at its fair. It was a mobile church, sponsored by the local United Methodists. The project was so successful that the laymen who directed it made plans to use the church-on-wheels at other county fairs and regional centers.

The church was manned by fifty-five volunteers who distributed literature, sold copies of the popular edition of the Bible, *Good News for Modern Man,* and talked to individuals about the role of the church in the county. Inside the unit, movies and recorded talks on drugs and other relevant subjects were offered as well as personal counseling.

Leaders of the project found that the attitude and witness of the volunteers was more important than the literature distributed free. Pamphlets on drugs and sex moved the fastest.

Project directors, who included the minister of St. John's United Methodist Church, said that the response to the mobile church showed that church members are guilty of cloistering within the confines and security of walls made of brick and mortar.

70. Photographs of New Members

Mt. Olivet Church in North Lima, Ohio, takes a Polaroid photograph of every new family that unites with the church. With names attached, the pictures are fastened to a prominently placed bulletin board so that the congregation can acquaint themselves with the family. In addition, the new members have "buddies" assigned to them to look after them on Sunday morning, introduce them to members, and encourage their church attendance.

71. Hospital Leaflets Provide Aid for Pastors and Laymen

"Why me?" is a question often asked by one who suffers an accident or serious illness.

"So you are a new patient," is a greeting from the nurse, roommate, or aide. Perhaps you are not waiting patiently to find what it is all about.

If there is anxiety about where illness might lead, we are concerned with dealing with our fears. And when the situation is rugged, the family wonders what to do with their troubles.

There is a good deal of loneliness in a time of serious illness. No one is certain about the faith that overcomes fear, but there is no one who does not seek the faith and pray that this conflict can be creative.

We want to learn how the pastor can help, so when he comes to the bedside, we do not miss an opportunity to be forthright.

These are the subjects of a few of the forty leaflets in the *Comfort and Strength* series. Order from 1720 Chouteau Ave., St. Louis, Missouri 63103.

72. No Magic Formula

In baptizing 115 persons last year to pace the Christian Churches (Disciples of Christ), the First Christian Church of Moline, Illinois, used no hocus-pocus—just the fundamentals of evangelism.

Successful evangelism involves primarily doorbells and shoe leather—and an interest in individuals that brings the church to a face-to-face confrontation with people as they are and where they are.

Lay people at First Christian Church do much of the calling which is basic to perpetual evangelism. People convene monthly to consider the prospect cards and distribute them among the department members. They, in turn, make their calls—with the department chairman keeping close check. If a call has not been made by a certain time, the chairman contacts the caller.

The core of the department's membership is persons who have special interests in evangelism and who have been doing this kind of work for years. One man has been influential in the past fifteen years in bringing more than four hundred people into the life and service of the church.

Training of callers consists mainly of sending them out in the company of seasoned visitors. Except for rather perfunctory training—filmstrips, role-playing, and a brief instructional period—the new callers learn by doing.

Some evangelism calls—often those in which decisions are finalized—must be made by one of First Church's three ministers.

While the congregation has no requirement about prospective members taking a course in church membership, such classes are offered throughout the year.

Resistance to the church's evangelistic outreach is present in Moline as elsewhere. The sophisticated person tends to resist participation in experiences which, to him, seem a little primitive. Also widespread is the growing desire of people not to become involved in anything outside themselves.

To overcome these defenses, the church carries on a highly personalized evangelism. The church has found that a poor record in evangelism can't be blamed on a shortage of potential members, who are everywhere.

A possible reason many congregations do not grow is because their ministers and departments are sitting in meetings wondering why the church is not growing instead of doing something about it. It is not a matter of lack of potential. It would seem to be more a matter of lethargy, indifference, and defeatism.

73. Try Renewing Membership Commitments Annually

An annual renewal of the individual's church membership to keep it in good standing is an idea being discussed in some Lutheran and other church circles.

"The key feature to this approach," writes United Press's religion editor Louis Cassells, "is that each member would have to decide once a year whether he wished to remain in or withdraw from the church. Unless he took positive action to renew his membership and commitment, he would be dropped."

No judgment would be made on the dropouts. It is hoped that they would not be forgotten but encouraged to find their way into the life of the congregation again.

74. How to Attract New Members

A local church should have 50 to 70 percent of its active membership on a responsibility list—everyone should have a task, and the church should know the special skills and talents of its members.

Then you can seek out new members. But before bringing new members into a church, you have to find them. Once the unchurched are discovered, they become the re-responsibility of your congregation. But how and where can prospective members be found?

1. Take a religious census. This is best undertaken by the council of churches or by all the churches in a small town.
2. Take an area survey with the church as the center, counting noses in all directions within the church's sphere of influence.
3. Check the church school enrollment to learn where parents of children belong to church.
4. Register church attendance.
5. During the time of pastoral services—such as weddings —invite the couple to join the church.
6. Alert members to spot recent arrivals in the community and to invite these new neighbors to church.
7. Seek out visitors at church socials, congregational meetings, and gatherings of a secular or civic nature.
8. Check with community agencies—Welcome Wagon, public utilities, etc.

9. In daily contacts with persons in the neighborhood and community, invite a nonchurch person to attend services with you.

75. Improve Your Church Newsletter

Your church news publication provides an opportunity to reach every member of your congregation—those who attend church and those who do not. A great many churches now produce a weekly or monthly newsletter, mimeographed or printed.

Production guidelines

Mimeographing is the least expensive. An electric typewriter will produce clear and clean copy. Regardless of how you reproduce your newsletter, keep these points in mind:

1. Design a permanent, attractive masthead for the front page. It should include the name of the paper, the name and address of your church, and the symbol of the denomination.
2. Elsewhere in the newsletter there should be a box or paragraph with the names of the pastor, music director, and the telephone number of the church office. List the name and telephone number of the newsletter's editor.
3. Some churches select a colored paper stock to distinguish their newsletters from other mail. Keep in mind that white or light green is the best background for readability.
4. Place the most important items on the first page.
5. Keep stories short. A two- or three-page piece will be skipped over by the reader.
6. Follow the principles of newswriting as if you were preparing copy for the local papers.

Content suggestions

Here are some suggestions for building interest into your newsletter:

1. Include a "letters to the editor" column.
2. Run profile pieces on members who lead interesting lives.
3. Print a sick list of members in the hospital.
4. Scatter short "did you know?" items throughout the newsletter.
5. Include stories about other churches in your area to which your members are invited.
6. Cull items from your denominational paper.
7. Try a column by the choir director for explaining new hymns, history of the anthem, and what the choir is planning in the way of special music.
8. Stories about a special feature of the church are interesting: rare window, Bible, etc.
9. A personal column on the minister and members who are participating in national or conference events.
10. News reports of things to come and actions taken by the church and its organizations.
11. Pro and con editorials, side by side, on controversial subjects.

To gain further ideas it is good to trade newsletters with other churches, your association, and your conference. In that way you share news as well as learn to improve your own publication.

76. Put Your Bulletin Boards to Work

Too many church bulletin boards are exhibiting a poor form of evangelism. As one views the yellowing pictures, the out-of-date information, and unkempt arrangements, these bulletin boards seem to say, "We don't care very much."

Yet every bulletin board offers a medium for creativity and imagination if a few simple suggestions are followed:

1. Set up a display area in the narthex combining the uses of the traditional bulletin board and the literature table. It should be located and designed to quickly catch the attention of members as they enter and leave the church.

2. Change the display at regular intervals, and illustrate events and ideas important to the life of the congregation.

3. Use photographs of members and church school pupils in action—at meetings, work projects, and other events in the life of the church. Appoint an official photographer to supply candids for display.

4. Display materials need not be elaborate. Use posters by church school members, displays from community organizations, materials from stewardship councils or committees, good quotations, etc.

5. Set one part of your bulletin board aside for the "smile section." Post cartoons, anecdotes, church humor. This can be an attention-getter for the more serious and personal items.

77. How to Greet Your Guests

The character of your church is shown by the way you treat strangers on Sunday morning.

Unfortunately, cold receptions are offered by many churches throughout the country. To remedy the situation, three keys to friendliness are offered:

Ministers. In your own way and words, always welcome

visitors from the pulpit. Be at the exit after the service to greet them personally.

Deacons. Be on hand before the service to spot new faces and extend your greetings. Invite them to sign a guest book or visitor card. During the following week, thank them for coming and encourage them to return.

Members. Look for a stranger seated near you. He or she may be a guest or a member you do not know. It makes no difference. After the service, instead of rushing out or talking to your friends, go up to the visitor, introduce yourself, and make him or her feel welcome.

78. Make the Telephone Work for You

A Conference call is a service provided by telephone companies. It is possible to make a conference call to several people at once. Some ministers have used this system to telephone their sermons "live" to sick parishioners. Consult the telephone company about costs and hookups. Price is about what some parishes pay for flowers.

Hotlines and lifelines. Many community groups across the country have established hotlines on which troubled teens, potential suicides, pregnant women, lonely persons can call to get help, advice, referrals, or simply the sound of a warm voice.

Typical is the Gulf Coast Help Line in Biloxi, Mississippi. The phones are manned by volunteers. The goal is to provide aid in finding available services for those who need them.

79. Evangelism Program Designed for Churches

An evangelism program can be aggressive, open, and

passionate. At the same time, it can be rational, positive, direct, and compelling. Here are some suggestions:

1. New congregations fostered by existing churches. They could be served by the pastors from the parent bodies. Such new congregations would not need to separate from existing churches.

2. "House churches" among persons not currently related to existing congregations. These house churches could be encouraged by "attached evangelists" who would be supported by existing churches.

3. Invitations to diverse folk to participate in the life of existing congregations. We need to be more aggressive and open in our offers to others to join with us.

4. Congregations formed around specific issues. Any idea that excites people can generate another church—some persons are now involved in a church dedicated to welfare rights.

5. Religious consciousness-raising. We must realize that developing new congregations does not imply a church building, but it does indicate the creation of groups of persons who gather to celebrate the gospel, to hear the Word, and to observe the sacraments.

80. Recorded on Film

St. Luke's Church in Dayton, Ohio, has a professional photographer in the congregation who kept a film account of the ministry. Six years of camera work have been condensed into a thirty-minute film titled "The St. Luke Story." This has proved excellent for use in church meetings, community clubs, and stewardship solicitations to depict graphically the challenging ministry of the church.

Holy Days and Holidays

81. Visuals Prominent in New Year Church Program

At the start of the new year, the Church of the Redeemer in New Haven, Connecticut, had a service they called "Worship Service of the Old and the New." The service summed up the activities of the year and pointed to new projects.

The congregation first viewed a 16mm movie made by children of the church school. The subject was Moses and the Ten Commandments. The film, made in the local park, was authenticated by the building of a golden calf and the breaking of the tablets.

An oral and illustrated report by young people followed. They described shoveling mud, rebuilding houses, and generally helping to clean up Wilkes-Barre, Pennsylvania, following the 1972 flood. Photographs were then shown of the cottage meetings held prior to the church's November stewardship drive. Following the reports, the participants dedicated their pledges, then formed small groups to discuss hopes for the church during the new year.

82. Havoc on Holiday Weekends

With the advent of the official three-day holiday, new problems of church attendance enter the scene. In Oxford, Connecticut, one of the churches is experimenting with a Thursday night service. Prior to Labor Day, Washington's Birthday, Memorial Day, and the Fourth of July, the service is held on Thursday evening at 8:00 P.M. The Sunday morning service is cancelled. The night attendance was double that of Sundays on the former long weekends.

83. A Dinner with a Purpose

During Lent a midwestern church had a fellowship supper to give an indication how much of the world goes to bed hungry. The sacrificial meal began at 6:45 P.M. At a cost of one dollar, each person present received a half-bowl of rice, a spoonful of broth over it, and a cup of unsweetened tea. Those who participated were asked not to eat a large lunch, but only a sandwich; they were also asked not to eat anything until breakfast the next day. The dollar was given to overseas relief. During the meal thoughts, prayers, feelings, and concerns were shared about hunger in the world.

84. Church Reenacts the Palm Sunday Triumphal Entry

Kindergarten teachers at St. Paul's Church in St. Paul, Minnesota, noted the children's interest in Jesus' triumphal entry into Jerusalem. One of the children said he knew a man who owned a donkey. So the teachers borrowed the animal and asked a church member to portray the Savior. The procession took place in front of the church with the children, ages four to twelve, carrying palm branches and lining the road.

85. Good Friday at the Mall

A pastor read George MacLeod's command to raise the cross in the marketplace as well as on the church steeple. Out of this experience, five ministers of Louisville, Kentucky, conceived and produced what they called a "Good Friday Happening."

The cross was raised in one of the busiest marketplaces in the city—the Mall. Participating in the service were members of Louisville's artistic community. The result was the fusing of music and dance with a dramatic recitation.

One participant read "Bad Friday" from Carl Burke's *God Is for Real, Man* and a prayer by Roman Catholic Michael Quoist. At the beginning and end of the presentation, the Motet Singers offered selections. As they sang, three members of the Louisville Civic Ballet danced out their interpretation of the words.

86. A Balloon Celebration

First and Calvary Presbyterian Churches in Springfield, Missouri, celebrated Christ's Resurrection with balloons on

Easter. Children in grades one through eight gave thought to the meaning of the Resurrection and wrote messages on balloons during the church school hour. Then they carried the balloons into the sanctuary along with their "One Hour of Sharing" offerings. They walked up the aisles and placed their offerings on the communion table and then came down and filled the aisles. After the benediction they led the congregation outside to release their balloons, sending messages of Easter gladness out into the world:

"The Lord Is Risen!" "Peace." "Smile—God Loves You." "Easter Joy." "Christ Lives!" "Love Is Victor." "Alleluia!" "Christ Has Set Us Free!"

It was a beautiful sight—the multicolored balloons sailing off into the deep blue sky over the smiling and laughing congregation.

87. Birthday Service Outdoors

First Community Church in Columbus, Ohio, celebrated Pentecost with an outdoor birthday service on a large grassy lot near the church. On that Sunday there was no other First Community worship service, as children of all ages were invited to participate with the adults. Worshipers were encouraged to arrive early for the celebration of the birth of the Christian church. Persons bringing banners were to arrive by 9:45 so they would have time to get their banners on poles.

Everyone was asked to stay by his parked car until the ushers signaled the beginning of the procession. The ushers signaled worshipers when to move toward the gathering area for the procession, which was introduced by a brass fanfare and led by a large Pentecost banner. The marchers peeled to the left and right to find seating when the group reached the seating area. Those with banners placed them in prepared holes.

Each person in attendance had been asked to bring with him a single flower; these had been collected by a "flower squad" of church school children, who carried them in the procession and placed them as decoration in front of the worship area.

The brief service included an outline of the original Pentecost story, a message by the minister, a reception of new members, breaking of the bread, and much singing.

No offering was taken during the service. However, offering baskets were available on the edge of the seating area. A congregational picnic followed the service.

88. Advent Preparation

In the North Haven (Connecticut) Congregational Church a tradition of long standing takes place on the first Sunday in Advent. The program begins at 4:00 P.M. and continues through the dinner hour, its purpose being to bring church families together, regardless of size or age, in preparation for and celebration of Christmas.

Each church school room becomes a craft shop. An adult "shopkeeper" assists in putting together or teaching a particular project. Simple ideas are used, things that can be done by children and completed in twenty minutes. Some of the projects are corsages, angels for a tree, mobiles, Christmas cards, tree ornaments, and window decorations. Following the craft period, a dinner is served in the fellowship hall. Milk and coffee are furnished, but each family brings its own box lunch.

79

One year a "mitten tree" was the center of decorations in the main hall. Each family brought a new pair of mittens to put on the tree. These were sent to a North Dakota Indian Reservation in time for Christmas.

89. Educational Greetings

At Immanuel Church in Cincinnati, the congregation does not send the minister's family a Christmas card. Instead, the price of the card is put into an envelope and placed on the offering plate or in a box in the vestibule during Advent. Personal greetings are still expressed, but the money is used for a lasting purpose; it is sent to a seminary to help a needy student who is studying for the ministry. This method of greeting contributes to the ongoing ministry of Christ as well as conveying good wishes to the pastor and his family.

90. One Card, Less Headache

The Corinth United Church of Christ in Hickory, North Carolina, has a Christmas card exchange that not only saves money to increase the benevolent fund but also helps the mailman. Instead of sending Christmas cards to fellow members of the church, each family brings one signed card to the sanctuary where it is placed in a conspicuous place with other cards. Thus the card becomes a holiday greeting to everyone in the congregation.

91. Stamped for Mission

What shall we do for Christmas this year? The question was asked at Central Church in Atlanta of a group interested in world missions. Someone suggested a display of Christmas postal stamps. A search turned up a great deal of interesting information and material for an eye-catching display of two hundred ninety-two stamps representative of forty-seven countries. Some eighty-eight countries have issued Christmas stamps. Madonna and child stamps were prominent in the display.

The stamps were carefully mounted on cards and identified by country. In some cases, interesting facts about particular stamps were added. The cards were then covered with clear wrap to protect them. They were arranged on a table, on boards, and on screens around a map of the world. Those of interest to children were placed low enough so they could be seen. Some of the United States stamps were shown with larger reproductions of the art, available from local museums or from the National Gallery of Art.

Christmas has meaning around the world because of Christian missions.

To help other churches interested in a similar display, three special lists are available on request: 1) a checklist of all Christmas stamps issued through 1971 (with Minkus and Scott numbers); 2) a list of art and artists identified on Christmas stamps; 3) the features and oddities of the Christmas stamps. Write to: Stewardship/Stamps, Box 29665, Atlanta, Georgia 30329.

Lay Fellowship

92. Ice Cream Supper Brings Togetherness

Zion United Church of Christ in Arthur, Illinois, has programs which emphasize family togetherness. For the annual ice cream supper, the families get together two days before the event to make ninety gallons of ice cream.

In addition, the church has a family night the first Sunday in Advent to decorate the church for Christmas. The Women's Fellowship makes articles for the local home for the aged and entertains the residents twice a year. Every summer, a family picnic is held in the park.

93. Pastoral Calling Through Small Groups

The pastor of the Community Church in Syosset, New York, has initiated a new program, a small group pastoral calling in his congregation of one thousand members. He has met evenings with ten to fifteen individuals in a lay person's home to discuss some of the significant areas of church life as it affects individual and family living.

The first phase of the program lasted eight months. Twenty-five sessions were held with 282 individuals in attendance. Since these represented families, 611 members of the congregation were indirectly involved.

"There were several things I liked about the meetings," remarked a member of the group. "There was no conversation dealing with superficialiaties of the day, but rather significant discussion on achieving commitment to the Gospel for today."

Out of the small group meetings, several new ideas developed. The pastor spent one day calling on ten commuters in their offices in Manhattan. During Lent, on the rear car of the 7:38 A.M. Syosset to Jamaica commuter train, he conducted experimental worship service aimed at catching the rhythm of the commuter. The service included hymn singing, a sermon, and prayers which focused on the competitive struggle in the world of work. A communion service ended the final day of the services.

94. Church Members Write Their Own Lenten Meditations

For Lent the members of First Congregational Church in Reading, Massachusetts, prepared their own meditations. Forty-seven members participated in the project. Their contributions, consisting of anecdotes, meditations, and original poetry joined with prayers, were mimeographed and distributed to the congregation.

A member of the church designed a booklet cover for the collection.

One of the meditations, written for Ash Wednesday, was prepared by a ninety-year-old former professor of mathematics.

95. How Lay People Can Share in Ministry

Immanuel United Church of Christ in Souderton, Pennsylvania, emphasizes a mutual ministry to involve everyone *in* the church in the work *of* the church. Here are the keys to the program:

1. Let everyone know that it is God who enables congregations to work together.
2. Take a biblically inspired approach—about one-quarter of Immanuel's members have taken part in small Bible study groups of about ten persons each.
3. Schedule every member for some responsibilities—members are automatically listed for ushering and greeting during the year.
4. Arrange avenues of service to one another—half the church women are involved in a group which tapes Sunday services for shut-ins, and each month a different couple serves as lay visitors, visiting all the sick and homebound at least once.
5. Involve everyone in worship—during Lent mother-daughter or father-son teams conducted Wednesday night services; during the summer a lay person assisted the visiting minister. (In a larger congregation more lay people could be involved in this.) Two lay people have total responsibility for worship services during the summer months.

6. Stimulate participation in running the church. Church committee membership is rotated so that all members, including young people, have a chance to serve.

When people have an opportunity to serve, they discover how God can direct them. Every church should try to create the mood and opportunity for mutual ministry.

96. A Covenant for Church Members

St. Andrews Church in Dexter, Michigan, has issued a covenant to help the members discuss current issues intelligently:

1. I will express as clearly as possible my position on the issue.
2. I will acknowledge the feelings that are generated in me by the various solutions to the issue.
3. I will listen to what other people feel and think about the issue.
4. I will seek to discover points of argument between myself and all others and will acknowledge points of difference between myself and others, seeking alternate solutions which might satisfy both sides.
5. I will concentrate on the issue as it relates to our area and not assume that what has happened somewhere else will happen where I live.
6. I will not make accusations which will discredit another person's character.
7. I will seek to resolve conflict in a way that moves people to genuine concern rather than to mere problem-solving.
8. I will try to be as concerned about those persons who are in conflict with me as about those persons who agree

with me. I will maintain the right of all persons to disagree with one another.

9. I will strive for a stronger sense of community to emerge between persons engaged in conflict because we have wrestled together on a common problem.

97. Encounter for Catholics

Families are brought together to solve their personal problems through a counseling program at St. Peter and Paul Catholic church in Miami, Florida. The family encounter movement has helped some two hundred families at weekend sessions. The program is not limited to members of the parish, or even to Catholics, but is Christocentric.

A typical weekend begins on Saturday morning with parents and their children meeting separately. Parents are asked to discuss the problems in their homes. The children meet with other young people.

At the end of the first day, the families are sent home to sleep but are asked not to discuss what happened. On Sunday the families return to the church for dialogue. Finally, each encounter ends with a worship service in which graduates of previous sessions join.

98. Decalogue for Parents

The United Church of Christ in Rootstown, Ohio, circulated a "ten commandments" for parents: (1) You will honor no other gods but GOD, steadfastly refusing to make your child a minor deity in your household. (2) You will make no promises that are broken, whether promises of pleasure or punishment; for unless a child learns to respect your word, he will not respect any person. (3) You will teach your child by example as well as precept. A parent who teaches a child religion and morality, but never goes to church, or lives by greed, passion, and self-indulgence must expect his conduct to be followed and his counsel ignored. (4) You will worship on the Lord's Day publically and communally, not seeking solitary pleasures which plunge each member of the family into social and spiritual isolation. (5) You will install no fears into your child, but impress on him the fact that perfect love casts out fear. He who pursues righteousness because of love is strong, but he who commits no wrongs out of fear, is weak. (6) You will help your child to accept the endless varieties of mankind with joy and wonder in God's creative originality, not breeding false pride. (7) You will not be overly protective, but allow a child to learn from his own mistakes. (8) You will not demand love simply because you are a parent, but will also try to earn love by being fair and just, with humor and understanding. (9) You will not force a child to develop into your own image, but will allow him to become the best kind of person his own nature permits. (10) You will look into your heart daily to examine your motives; impure motives curdle love and affection into mere possessiveness.

99. Caution: Men at Work

The Peoria Heights (Illinois) Congregational Church has had a successful men's program going for several years. The men meet on Wednesday evenings from 7:00 to 9:00 P.M. The first hour is spent on building maintenance; the second, in social activities talking, ping-pong, pool, cards, and drinking coffee. The program has served to strengthen the commitment to the church.

100. Women Can Change Life-Styles in Their Community

Women's groups in a church have an opportunity to discover frontiers of service in their community. This outward look comes after the earlier process of ministering to each other has begun. The goal of a guild or fellowship should be to learn about their community, to discover the needs, and then to respond to the situation. Here are some concrete projects that might be undertaken:

Open a combination women's activity and child care center. The staff can be chosen from all age groups and both sexes. The elderly should not be overlooked; they might welcome the opportunity to be with children. For the activity center, provide coffee, literature, books, and even a series of courses ranging from crafts to auto mechanics.

Many women have benefited from small group gatherings in which they could talk about their feelings, needs, and hopes. Provide child care and meet in a room away from a telephone.

Compile a directory of family service centers.

A women's fellowship can provide education for new types of life-styles, such as cooperative and communal living.

If there are women in your fellowship who would like to return to school, establish a fund to enable them to do so.

101. Retreat for Bereaved Persons

The Missouri Conference of the United Church of Christ offered a retreat for recently bereaved persons, motivated by the idea that the church does not do enough for those in sorrow.

The project was not a meeting of mourners but a joyous event in which sharing and concern came from individuals who had discarded their masks.

During the retreat there were discussions, periods of worship and meditation, activities and crafts, nature hikes and bird walks, music, and good food. There were also tears, but in the presence of love, healing began to take place.

102. Love Is Subject of Weekend Retreat

First Congregational Church in Berkeley, California, had a weekend retreat which they called "Nurturing in Love." This title was used because the aim of the retreat was to show the many ways love can be encouraged.

The event began on Friday evening with dessert, followed by several contemporary dramas. An intergeneration square dance enlivened the occasion.

On Saturday morning small groups gathered to react to the message of the dramas. After a luncheon, a panel of theologians discussed questions that related to the topic of love. Out of these discussions came a definition of sexuality.

Emphasis centered not only on a person's marital status but also on being human persons.

103. Association of Small Churches Overcomes Size Limitations

It is often a disappointment for the members of a small church to read about the many exciting ministries and projects of a large congregation. Small churches are usually limited to fewer programs.

However, twenty-six congregations in the rural Clarion Association of Penn West Conference have overcome the boxed-in feeling by providing a structure for leadership training and a variety of activities.

Activities in the association last year included: two choir festivals; an in-depth study of a small rural church school; two youth rallies; a cooperative week of meetings with a visiting missionary; distribution of mission publications and audio-visual youth materials; a listing of community action projects for small rural churches; an evangelism workshop on how to increase membership and be successful in neighborhood visitation; a pulpit exchange; and a dinner for church councils to show how their work can be enriched.

Four times a year a newspaper is mimeographed for distribution to all church members. In addition, dry annual reports of the association have been canned in favor of panel discussions reevaluating spiritual foundations. Task forces are studying the problem of drug abuse and the interpretation of denominational programs.

104. Small Groups Bring Vitality to Church in Massachusetts

"Ours is a transient and mobile suburb. It is common for me not to know my next door neighbor. Since people are always moving, I have been reluctant to establish friendships. As a result I often feel lonely," said one of the neighborhood residents to a member of a South Action, Massachusetts, church.

Acting on this widespread sentiment, the church created

opportunities for family experiences. Church members, especially new ones, are invited to join a small group. When twelve to fifteen show interest, they begin to meet together in the home of one member. Each miniature fellowship chooses its name, which reflects its distinctiveness—Clyde's Collection, Bonnie's Bunch, L. Group.

There is no established agenda for the meetings. Each small fellowship determines its own direction, projects, and pace. Initially, one person serves as leader, but eventually leadership becomes a function shared by the entire group.

Activities so far have included oceanside camping retreats, sensitivity exercises, a visitation program at a geriatric hospital, group storytelling, wine tasting, gourmet meals, theater parties, and midnight discussions centering on various personal, social, and theological issues.

105. Downtown Luncheons

Many churches have some sort of fellowship dinner, usually held in the evening. The United Presbyterian Church in Newark, New Jersey, sponsors a luncheon every Thursday in its fellowship hall. The cost per meal is seventy-five cents. Businessmen who attend can join a fifteen-minute worship service, which includes a brief message relating to the problems of the city or to personal difficulties.

The Glenview Community Church in Glenview, Illinois, has a downtown luncheon for its church members at 12:15 on Wednesdays. The program and meal take an hour. Usually some phase of the church's work is discussed.

Mission

106. Eight Ways to Highlight Mission Giving

Here are eight proven methods to help members of your congregation appreciate and support missions:

1. Have a lay person speak about his or her interest in mission at the Sunday worship service.
2. Pray regularly for missionaries, both publicly and privately—especially when you read about something they are doing.
3. Use banners, posters, and bulletin inserts with a mission theme.
4. Have a mission bulletin board, changing it regularly. Watch for good display pictures.
5. At a mission family night, invite church members who have traveled to bring slides for viewing.

6. Consider showing provocative mission films at the sermon time.
7. Make handcrafts from home or overseas missions available for sale.
8. Quote from missionary letters from the pulpit and in your parish newsletters.

For further information, write to Church World Service —SERV, Box 188, New Windsor, Maryland 21776.

107. Rock Pot Project Aids Mission Work

An eighty-year-old retired pastor and his wife in Worland, Wyoming, organized what they call a "Rock Pot Project." He gathers, cuts, and polishes interesting rocks which he finds in the area around his home, then uses them to decorate flower pots. First, he coats the pots with cement and then embeds the polished stones into the mortar. The decorated pots are offered for sale to tourists and people in the community.

The money received from the sale of the rock pots is sent to overseas missions.

Painters, lumbermen, and the town's citizens have contributed clear glaze, lumber, and pots to the project so that the whole community has become involved in this mission effort.

108. Bucket Brigade

Members of St. Paul's United Church of Christ in Lancaster, Pennsylvania, have gone the second mile in their support of Evangelical Hospital in Khairiar, India. Early in 1971, medical missionary Manfred Luan told the congregation about the needs of his one hundred-bed hospital that serves 250,000 persons from forty-six villages. St. Peter's budget was already adopted, but members put shiny brass buckets at each church door, and by December they had collected nearly three thousand dollars. Another $1,067 was given by July, 1972. Everyone at St. Peter's is happy with the project—especially those who have the joy of giving to a project which they consider very important.

109. Auction Your Talents

A novel way to develop a sense of community has been found by First Congregational Church in Wilmette, Illinois. A "time and talent auction" offered such jobs as baby-sitting, car washing, silver polishing, flower arranging, needlepoint lessons, preparing meals or desserts, tennis lessons, sailing lessons, ghost-writing articles, or preaching sermons. The money raised went to the church's outreach program.

110. Book for Mission

First United Church of Christ in Oroville, California, keeps a book just inside the sanctuary labeled *Mission*. The book, frequently updated, is a record of the accomplishments of the church in mission and the listing of the opportunities and challenges available.

111. Get First-Hand Reports

Dramatize your church's mission by inviting a missionary on furlough to speak at a worship service, family night, mission fest, or a special group meeting. Retired missionaries, as well as persons who have visited projects in the U.S. or overseas, also make good first-hand reporters.

112. Have a Mission Fest

The old-fashioned German "mission-fest" or the weekend for mission can provide your church with loads of fun and a better understanding of the church's work around the world. Here's how: Ask a committee—with a strong chairman—to set the date, arrange time and program, and plan for promotion, food, finances. An inspiring speaker, displays, music, and a children's program will help. Set a goal and announce how the offering will be used (special envelopes are worthwhile). Arrange for press and radio coverage before and during the event. If your mission fest includes a church homecoming, be sure to introduce guests and provide name tags for everyone.

Planning

113. Goal Setting Pays Big Dividends

Last fall Bethany United Church of Christ in Baltimore, Maryland, discovered that the planning process works in a suburban church.

In September, thirty key lay members spent a total of twelve hours as a group learning how the planning process and goal-setting system is used in industry, schools, and churches.

Two weeks later, twenty-five of the leaders returned to identify the needs, problems, and hopes of their congregation. Four priorities were set for the church, and participants volunteered for a task force related to one of the areas.

The four priorities were stewardship, Christian education, involvement in the world, and involvement of laymen at Bethany.

Progress has already been noted in interest, attendance,

income, and enthusiasm, which are higher than at any time in the last thirteen years.

114. Five Questions to Help You Evaluate Organization in Your Church

1. What are the stated and assumed goals, objectives, and priorities of your congregation or group?
2. How are decisions made, and how are problems solved? Who does what? Are the lay members and persons affected involved?
3. Do you have effective ways to communicate decisions, programs, and plans?
4. To what degree are leadership functions shared (professional and volunteer)? Are your expectations clear?
5. Do you work well together? Are feelings expressed freely and dealt with honestly? Do subgroups (committees, etc.) function as part of the whole and see common goals?

115. Five Ideas to Help You Improve Your Organizational Program

1. The task and the group are important. Each group has a task to accomplish and is composed of persons with needs. Corporate cohesion and personal enrichment are as important as the task.
2. Share the leadership. A group is more than leader and followers. The leader's skills and knowledge, together with the capacities of others, are required for effective activity.
3. Plan carefully.
4. Feelings are important. A disregard for personal relationships imperils decisions and weakens fellowship.

97

5. Use a consultant. Objective observation and comment on your goals and procedures will help you act on real purposes.

116. Plan for a Weekend Retreat

Decide why, when, and how to meet. Concentrate on one subject. Allow enough time for full and frank discussion. Take time for recreation. Provide an atmosphere of friendship and trust.

People

Make the size of the participating group manageable—perhaps only church officers and board or committee members. Include at least one outside leader to assure fresh viewpoints.

Don't spend the whole weekend traveling. But pick a place far enough away so no one can go home in the middle of the session. An informal setting isolated from other groups and distractions is ideal.

Plan

Friday: Brief evening vespers and presentation of theme. Free time for informal recreation.

Saturday: Morning sessions with coffee break. Afternoon session. Recreation. Evening session. Vespers. Singing and free time.

Sunday: Final session. Worship and communion at, or after, lunch.

117. No Bored Board

The Rock Spring Church in Arlington, Virginia, has seven effective steps for keeping their church board from becoming bored at the monthly meetings. (1) Agenda: the chairman knows what he wants to accomplish and informs the members. This requires thought beforehand. (2) Attendance: spotty attendance means spotty and ineffective board work. The secretary should contact members before meetings. This is especially necessary when specific meetings are held or changes are made in meeting times. (3) Plan specific programs of action: involve as many people as possible. (4) Minutes are not so much for the historical record as to remind everyone what has been decided and who agreed to what. (5) Follow through to see that assignments are completed. This especially is the function of the chairman and the secretary. (6) Keep the congregation informed by printing pertinent matters in the church newsletter or Sunday bulletin. (7) Be alert for capable new people to become part of the administrative aspect of the congregation. Seek new blood for special assignments.

118. Church Secretaries' Workshop

A church secretaries' workshop was recently held at First Church in Bristol, Connecticut, with forty people in attendance. A new dimension added to this year's program of sharing, fellowship, and study was that ministers of the participating secretaries were also present.

A short devotion began the day. The morning discussion centered on a series of "imagineering" games. The purpose of the games was to demonstrate the process of teamwork.

Following lunch the group divided into workshops—on newsletters, Sunday church bulletins, membership lists, directories, and annual reports. Each workshop provided for give-and-take, and participants moved from one subject group to another.

119. Questions to Evaluate a Project

History

How did it begin?

What has been accomplished?

Where has it failed?

Goals

What is the long-term goal?

What are this year's objectives?

Can the church afford it?

Is it worth it?

People

Who started it?

Are the initiators still involved?

Who makes the decisions?

Who does the work?

Who is being reached?

Is the community involved?

Place

Where does the project take place?

Are the facilities adequate?

Is this the best place?

120. Five Steps to Effective Planning

1. Assumptions. Check out the underlying premises upon which your program or plans are to be based.
2. Objectives. Establish the target(s) or goal(s) toward which the specific action is directed.
3. Strategy. Devise a general course of action to achieve your objectives.
4. Tactics. Select the most promising steps to be taken to implement the strategy.

5. Evaluation. Take a "dip-stick" check to determine whether strategy and tactics are achieving your objectives. If necessary, modify your approach.

Planning is an on-going process. It is never completed but should be part of the life-style of any effective organization.

121. Task Forces Can Accommodate Differing Views

The First Parish in Lincoln, Massachusetts, has discovered some underlying values and procedures which support task forces. They are:

1. Each person is entitled to his own views about people and the world.
2. No social issue can, or should be expected to, find full support in any social organization.
3. The right to oppose an issue is as valid as the right to support it—opposition should not be the cause of guilt feelings.
4. But any person who is motivated to act on an issue through the church should feel free to do so through a task group—opposition by some should not kill efforts by others.
5. First Parish's committee of concern helps individuals and groups implement and act on issues. It supplies money and manpower to groups and educates the parish about human suffering and need at home and throughout the world.

Organizing the ideas

The First Parish now houses four task groups—peace, education, prison reform, and concern on the need for adult social contacts. The development of the prison reform group illustrates how to organize people.

1. One woman active in penal reform set up a series of discussions on the subject for the senior high Pilgrim Fellowship.
2. Inspired, the youths created and supplied a library for a nearby prison, educating the general congregation in the process.
3. A concerned member of the congregation, spurred by prison uprisings, found a respected church and community leader to chair a task group.
4. The group organized three educational seminars for the parish, inviting prominent people in prison work and concerns to speak.
5. As a result of the seminars, the membership of the group increased.
6. As another response to the seminars, the task force pushed to aid the passage of legislation on prison reform, and one member became a watchdog on the progress of the legislation.
7. The prison reform group is now exploring ways to support existing private and public rehabilitation efforts.

Membership in the task groups tends to be small. There is no pressure to increase their number. This helps assure that only committed individuals work on the projects. It also allows several groups to exist, covering a broad area of social action.

122. Self-Evaluation Questions for a Congregation

1. Is there an openness to the power of the Holy Spirit? Do the members believe, and act on the belief that God is at work today?
2. Is there a strong personal orientation in the life, pro-

gram, ministry, and outreach of the congregation? Is the primary motivating force a desire to meet the needs of people, or does it concentrate on getting people to participate in "our program"?

3. Is the basic orientation toward the future?

4. Are there clearly defined, positive expectations about tomorrow?

5. Is corporate worship recognized as a central and crucial element in the life of the congregation? Is worship seen as a vital experience for the Christian, or is it viewed as an obligation inherited from the past?

6. Is the definition of the purpose of the church clearly stated and widely understood? Does it unify or divide the membership? Or has the definition of the purpose, role, and mission of your parish never been articulated?

7. Do the members trust one another? Do they trust the pastor? Does the pastor trust the members? Is there a depth of trust that enables people to work together despite differences on tactics or on priorities?

8. Is the base of participation and involvement growing? Is the proportion of members involved in making the decisions and carrying out the ministry of the parish larger this year than it was last year?

9. Is there a recognition that the parish has obligations to each member?

10. Has anything new been added to the program and ministry of the parish in the past year?

Social Service

123. To Pep Up the Sick

A member of a Baptist church recalled that when she was ill, the women's fellowship gave her a memorable gift. It was a seed catalog, but clipped to the cover was an envelope containing an order blank and a check made out to the seed company. She read the catalog page by page and made endless lists and planned dozens of imaginary gardens before she filled the order.

Since then, the fellowship has used appropriate catalogs with great success. To a teen-age girl goes a costume jewelry pamphlet, to a young boy a sports catalog, to a fisherman a listing of trout flies or other fishing equipment.

The secret is to learn the hobby of the person in the sickbed and then take it from there.

124. Counseling Services

St. Peter's Church in Elmhurst, Illinois, established a ministry of counseling services. A minister was added to the staff to focus on the individual, the marriage, and the family. All persons are welcome to use these services. Such a form of ministry reflects the concern of the religious community for the psychological and spiritual well-being in contemporary man.

In addition, the program provides selective referral. If a pastor is uncertain as how to help an individual in the best way, the counseling service can conduct an initial interview. On the basis of this interview, if it is determined that the individual could be helped by more intense or specialized treatment, referral is made to the agency or professional facility best suited to his particular need.

The counseling services are also available to ministers who feel the need for personal consultation in regard to their own lives or to their pastoral relationships.

125. Ethics in the City

A business and ethics seminar was conducted by the Hingham (Massachusetts) Congregational Church in downtown Boston. The seminar was for church members who work in the city. The men and women wrestled with the difficulties of Christian decision-making in the complex milieu of modern business life. The seminar meets for a six-week period in the spring and fall.

126. Religion and the Parking Lot

The cooperation of a city-wide parking lot firm, members of the three main religious bodies, and a responsive public has resulted in a no-overhead project which has been bene-fitting Washington, D. C.'s urban poor.

Called "ProJeCt," an acronym for "Protestant, Jew, Catholic," the loosely organized venture has collected several tons of canned and packaged foods during six-week periods for distribution to churches and other agencies working with people in need.

The encouraging results of ProJeCt have been due to the involvement of personnel at the parking lots of Parking Management, Inc. The firm printed posters and fliers urging its customers to bring in nonperishable foods and deposit them in specially marked bins at the parking lots.

On Fridays, PMI employees collect the food and take it to a center, where it is sorted for distribution to such agencies as Fides Neighborhood House, Lutheran Social Services Food and Clothing Center, Zaccheus Community, and others.

Working to keep the venture—which involves several parking lots around the city—functioning smoothly is a group of laymen and clerics—Catholic, Protestant, and Jewish—who get together at noon once a week for discussion.

127. What's Happening Here?

There was unused clothing in the Clothes Closet filled by Mt. Pleasant Lutheran Church women in Saluda, South Carolina. And there were school children needing clothing. So the women went into action.

By appointment and through the recommendation of schools and community agencies, they found out which children and families needed clothing. The task, however, was overwhelming, and surpassed the womanpower of the LCW.

Assistance was asked of other churches, organizations, and citizens. In three months, 350 persons had received at least eight garments each, along with underwear, shoes, and accessories. More than one thousand volunteers worked on a one-to-one basis.

Women began to realize there was a second problem— the system did not support people's dignity. Moreover, the operation had outgrown the church school rooms at Mt. Pleasant.

They decided to incorporate. The newly formed Saluda Community Center opened with a thrift shop for its members. Membership is granted to individuals or family units of Saluda County who qualify for aid by standards set by the Center. Standards are based on the U.S. government's schedule for the free lunch program, which benefits persons considerably above what has been set as the poverty level.

A membership "credit" card is given each family group, entitling each family member to all services of the center. During a six-month period families may spend up to six dollars for each child under twelve and eight dollars for those over twelve.

Each item in the shop has a token price: dresses, fifteen cents to seventy-five cents; children's clothing, five cents to fifty cents, for example. At present 130 families, totalling more than nine hundred persons, hold membership. In addition, immediate service is given to fire victims, transients, and victims of natural disasters, regardless of income and without charge if necessary.

Profits are used by the center to hire members for mending and sorting clothings, to send children of members to summer camp, to provide education and cultural enrichment programs or emergency services.

The Saluda Community Center is the first nonsectarian, biracial community-involved corporation of its kind in Saluda County. St. Paul's Methodist Church has leased their old eight-room, two-story parsonage to the center rent free.

128. Newspaper Gives Confidence

The Roberts Center Light, a casual and lighthearted effort in amateur newspaper journalism, has appeared on the Boston College campus. The paper is the work of some sixty handicapped youngsters, eighteen years old and younger, who have found it a means to gain confidence and incentive in confronting some of the difficult problems of life. The children are students at the Campus School of the Jesuit university and at the nearby Children's Hospital. Getting rid of labels in their own minds is one of the problems the young people have upon first entering school. Although each child has a handicap (deafness, emotional disturbance, physical handicap), these are minimized. The newspaper has helped build confidence and faith.

129. Foster Home

The Church Women United group in Akron, Ohio, organized a committee for the purpose of finding foster homes for youngsters who are in the care of the Summit County Juvenile Court. The church leaders found that many young people detained by the court needed to be placed in foster homes rather than being incarcerated in a detention situation. Healthy family living and love was, as the court expressed, the therapy which many of the youths needed.

130. Blanket Sunday

Zion Church in Peru, Illinois, has a Sunday when blankets are displayed throughout the sanctuary. These are hung on the walls, from the pulpit, and on the altar. The blankets are made during a particular month in the church. Men and women wash, cut, and sew squares together, line the blanket, and knot each square. Each Thursday they meet to work, enjoying a potluck dinner at mealtime. The project promotes fellowship. The blankets are donated to emergency relief programs. This plan is especially suited for mixed groups, retired individuals, or the aged.

131. Society Offers Aid for Groups Planning Day Care Program

"A good day care program is the first step toward a better life for children, families, employers, and the whole community." This statement appears in a brochure that describes a day care consultation service available to community groups, churches, and institutions through the Bensenville, Illinois, Home Society.

The brochure asks who needs day care. It answers the question by citing four groups that do—children and families, churches, employers, and communities.

Another question is what can be done. Some of the suggested steps are:

Survey community needs.

Learn about a good day care program.

Educate the community.

Issue position papers on matters relating to day care.
Raise money for support.
Start a day care program.

132. Church Gives Counseling Center
to Town as Gift

The Rehoboth Congregational Church in Rehoboth, Massachusetts, gave a gift of appreciation to the town which has supported and benefited from its ministry for over 250 years. At a special meeting of the church, members voted to support the Rehoboth Problem Solving Center.

Serving as the initiating group for the project was the 250th anniversary committee of the church which worked out the details with the Massachusetts Department of Mental Health. A member of the department will serve as executive secretary for the new center.

The project will involve many persons throughout the community, both professionals and laymen, who are receiving special training from the state to equip them to counsel families and individuals. Teams of three or four "community care-givers" will work with those seeking advice. Consultants will also be available from the department of mental health.

A fifteen-member board of directors will be responsible for the control of the new organization.

133. Lentil and Rice Meal Given
to Raise Money for Refugees

"Where's the salad?" a teenager asked as he picked up his plate of rice and lentils. The answer was simple, "No salad tonight."

Then an adult looked up from his portion of rice and lentils wondering, "What is there to drink?" "Water, if you want it," came the reply.

Community Church in Oklahoma City was having a sacrificial meal for the people of Bangladesh. If churches care to have a sacrificial meal, here is the way to prepare the rice and lentils. Many persons at Community Church liked the dish so well that they asked for the recipe.

Dal (lentils prepared to eat with boiled rice)

2 cups lentils
6 cups water
1 teaspoon salt

Boil over low heat until lentils are soft. Stir until well mixed; it should be fairly thick.

1 medium onion, thinly sliced
½ teaspoon turmeric
½ teaspoon ginger
1 teaspoon cumin seed

Sauté slightly in oil, add spices, and sauté for a minute or two. Add to lentils. Mix well. Serve over plain boiled rice.

134. Ten Commandments Offered to Church Volunteers by Social Workers

A guide for volunteers in general—including those who give their time and energies to church work—has been prepared by Daniel Thursy, dean of the University of Maryland school of social work.

Congressman Keith G. Sebelius (R-Kan.) inserted the "Ten Commandments for Volunteers" into the *Congressional Record* because he believes that the volunteer worker "is the backbone of most organizations."

Dr. Thursy's guide will help improve your church organizations, church schools, and community efforts. Here are the steps:

1. Understand the job you undertake.
2. Accept training appreciatively, contributing your own experience.
3. Match your interests to the job's needs as well as your own.
4. Serve faithfully and report new insights about your work.
5. Discover its meaning to the total program of which it is a part.
6. Open yourself to opportunities for growth in skill, sympathy, self-confidence, and responsibility.
7. Value your special two-way role as a community interpreter.
8. Contribute to supervision by self-evaluation and a willingness to ask.
9. Give loyalty to your institution and its program.
10. Take pride in the volunteer's career. It pays handsomely in treasures of the spirit.

135. Investment in Hope

Members of St. Mark's Episcopal Church in Foxboro, Massachusetts, have created a fund to help persons who face unforeseen crises. The "Building Life Fund" does not require canvassing. All money is spontaneously contributed. The fund makes it possible to stand behind people who need help.

136. How to Prepare for Racial Change

At Messiah United Church of Christ in Baltimore, the congregation is groping its way through the process of racial transition in response to the promptings of conscience and spirit. At each definitive step some members become uneasy, but so far everyone has stayed with the church. Here are some steps they have taken:

1. The congregation debated and adopted a resolution on open membership when the neighborhood began to change.
2. They opened the church buildings to community groups —a city health department unit operates a baby clinic; there are AA and Al-Anon chapters and a community organization group. The congregation is actively involved.
3. They used part-time personnel and volunteers in community ministry.
4. They try to keep the whole congregation informed about changes taking place in the church and neighborhood.
5. They try to utilize the skills of everyone in the church for work in the community.
6. Leaders of the congregation meet frequently to discuss the process and to evaluate the progress.
7. They try to deal with opposition creatively and openly without judging those who move more slowly.
8. They pray for guidance.

137. Colorado Churches Provide Assistance to Fifteen Thousand Migrants

What can churches do for migrants who move through their areas? In seven sections of Colorado there is a migrant ministry that might serve as a model.

The Colorado Migrant Ministry is a cooperative program of twelve denominations for the fifteen thousand migrants who travel each year in the agricultural areas of the state. Most are Spanish-speaking Americans. Others are Navajo or Sioux Indians and black farm workers from the southern states.

Among the Colorado Migrant Ministry's many projects and concerns are:

1. Assistance in day care nurseries in cooperation with local church groups.
2. Recreational programs.
3. Transportation for migrants to doctors, clinics, or hospitals.
4. Housing and health improvement projects.
5. Library programs in which books, games, and toys are loaned or given to migrant children.
6. Family counseling.
7. Community relations programs.
8. Vacation Bible schools in Protestant and Roman Catholic churches.
9. Community leadership development among migrants.

Father Gregor Dues of the Pueblo Diocese of the Roman Catholic Church in Colorado has prepared a curriculum for use with migrant children. The booklet, "Handbook for Church Migrant Programs," has been used by Catholics and Protestants for religious instruction. For further program suggestions write to the Colorado Council of Churches, 1313 Clarkson Street, Denver, Colorado 80218.

Stewardship

138. Seed Money for Projects

Parkway Church in Minneapolis, Minnesota, is a merger of two churches—Fremont Avenue and Pilgrim Heights Congregational Churches. The Fremont church was sold for fifty thousand dollars. The money was invested so that income would be available to support the Newcomer Project of the Upper Midwest Indian Center, which was faltering because of lack of support. The project can now provide temporary housing and guidance for Indian families moving from Standing Rock Indian Reservation into the twin cities. An Indian family is provided housing for up to three months. The husband is assisted in finding work, the children are enrolled in school, and the mother is given help in adjusting to urban life. Permanent housing is then found for the family, and a new family enters the orientation program.

139. Posting the Givers

First Christian Church in Alliance, Ohio, posted a list of the names of individuals who made pledges toward the operation of the church program. The size of the pledge was not listed. The purpose of the list, which was posted on the wall in the narthex of the church, was to indicate who could be counted on to help with responsible planning and action in the mission of the congregation.

140. The Lord's Acre

While not new, the Lord's Acre plan is still worth trying in rural areas where small churches might be struggling to make ends meet. Several decades ago, the Reverend Dumont Clarke became the pioneer of a plan to help churches in the Smoky Mountains. The men and women of a church leased a field or secured free acreage and then plowed, fertilized, planted, cultivated, and harvested the crop in a cooperative way. The entire receipts of the crop were given to the church.

Variations are possible with the Lord's Acre program. In Vermont a farmer in the church gave out seed potatoes to be turned into a fall crop for the church school. Another example was an egg farmer who gave all the eggs his hens laid on Sundays to the church to sell and use the funds for their treasury.

141. Developing Talents

How do you stimulate a church to develop its talents? This question concerned members of the Easthampton Congregational Church (Massachusetts). An anonymous group in the church raised seventy-five dollars to take out a three-month bank loan for three thousand dollars. They contacted the minister and informed him they would like to loan this money to the church interest-free for three months providing the money would be used as a talent project to help the church develop its potential.

The project was approved by the church council, and one Sunday morning each member of the congregation was handed a crisp ten-dollar bill. The minister preached a sermon on the parable of the talents. Each member then put his ten dollars to work by investing in some kind of project—crafts, selling a gourmet dinner, publishing poetry, etc. After three months the talent money was recalled; the $3,000 had grown to $7,700. While the amount of talent money was notable, new talent and community spirit also emerged.

142. Task Force Builds Interest in Finances and Membership

On the first Tuesday of each month, a task force gathers at St. Andrew's Church in Buffalo to plan programs in community service, membership care and cultivation, building maintenance, and special fund-raising projects.

The task force was an outgrowth of several efforts to stem the decline in church membership and to increase concern over the financial programs of the congregation.

When the church council presented the problem to the

congregation, cutting back services was rejected as a solution to the doldrums of the church. Instead, sixty persons signed up to see what could be done to stir up enthusiasm. At the first meeting, thirty-two individuals were present. They divided into four groups—fund-raising, membership, program, and maintenance. These groups decided to meet on a monthly basis and invited others to attend. The first suggestion was a Christmas sacrificial offering—so as to begin the New Year without any debt. This offering came to over one thousand dollars.

Since then, the task force has awakened the congregation to a vital interest in the church program. During Lent another fifteen hundred dollars was raised in self-denial envelopes. Inactive members were visited and urged to attend services; attendance was recorded.

Forums on income tax preparation, wills, drug abuse, and college choices were available to the community.

The maintenance task force sponsored a clean-up and painting campaign. Sixty-five gallons of paint were applied in the building by church members.

The most encouraging signs have been the participation of the youth. High school young people lead the groups on finances and program. They work along with the adults rather than as a separate group.

143. How Michigan Church Oversubscribed Its Budget

The budget of a Chelsea, Michigan, church was oversubscribed by 10 percent this year after a systematic program of stewardship interpretation. A nine-member committee began by setting a time, talent, and treasure budget and by enlisting a group of capable persons to work as counselor-canvassers.

The counselor-canvassers were thoroughly trained prior to Loyalty Sunday and several informative letters were sent to member families. Each family or member was assigned to a counselor-canvasser.

During the sermon time on three successive Sundays, an audiovisual presentation described what the church was doing in its community, in the nation, and across the world.

Following each service, the members were invited to the fellowship hall for coffee and doughnuts. During an informal period the members and their counselor-canvassers discussed the church's program and financial needs for the coming year.

The counselor-canvassers met at lunch on each of the Sundays to review progress. On the third Sunday the canvassers visited members who had not attended the discussion sessions. A special youth team met with teen-agers to discuss their pledges to the church.

144. Rock Around the Clock

In St. Thomas, Ontario, sixteen girls spent twenty-four hours in rocking chairs to raise money for the Bonne Bay, Newfoundland, Mission. Sponsors contributed an agreed amount for each hour rocked. They earned $217 and enjoyed reading, watching TV, and playing floor hockey while they continued the rocking marathon.

145. Double-Edged Mower

From spring through fall the members of a church in Arlington, Virginia, mow the church lawn and care for the grounds. Organizing their own crews of three or more, the men and women make quick work of it and enjoy themselves too. The result puts a double edge on stewardship. Besides saving money to be used in other ways, the members have demonstrated their practical concern for care and maintenance of property.

146. Beating Inflation

To meet its budget and beat inflation, a California church has taken four steps to cut costs: (1) a less expensive method is used for printing the newsletter. (2) Postage bills were cut by mailing only essential items. (3) Telephone toll calls have been avoided and a public telephone disconnected. (4) Members have been asked to use church resources conscientiously. The church hopes that by cutting back on its expenses it can avoid trimming its contributions for national and international programs.

147. Sing Them Over Again

Frank Godley, the organist at Lundy's Lane United Church, Niagara Falls, Ontario, played more than five hundred hymn tunes in a six-and-a-half hour "hymnathon." More than three hundred dollars was contributed by church members for the chancel choir's music fund.

148. Questions at Budget-Building Time

When your church board sets out to build a budget, be sure to face questions like these: What are the goals of our congregation? What do we value most highly? How are we serving our members, our community, and our world this year? How much income can we count on—from all sources? How much will the fixed expenses (fuel, electricity, insurance etc.) increase? How much should we increase the salaries of the minister and staff? How much should we allocate for emergency repairs? What new equipment do we need and can we afford? What percentage of our total budget should we allocate for missions? What new programs or new community efforts should we undertake? How can we keep the members of our congregation informed about our total mission? What controls and evaluation methods are necessary to keep the cash flow constant and to stay within our income?

149. The Pony Express

To dramatize its annual stewardship drive, the Mamrelund Lutheran Church in Kent City, Michigan, set up a "pony express" system. On a designated Sunday, members were asked to make their pledges for the coming year. As one member completed his pledge card, he took the pouch full of cards to his neighbor who filled out his own card and went on to the next family. The pony express relay went on until the circuit was complete. Of course, many people used automobiles; others went on foot. But several persons made the trip on real ponies. Members of the committee found that the idea saved a lot of work, speeded up the canvass, and created a good bit of excitement among the congregation for the enlistment campaign.

150. Pesetas Flow in When Boys Cut Long Hair

Long hair is "in" in the small town of Argamasilla de Alba, Spain, at least for the young people. But two young cousins there, Joaquin and Candido Lanzarote, decided to make the "supreme sacrifice" if it would help the church building fund. They informed local newsmen that they'd "shave their heads to the bone" if townspeople would donate seven hundred dollars. Joaquin and Candido staged a "shave-in," reached their goal, and have very short hair for the moment.

151. One Way of Fund Raising

"Give until it hurts" has been a fund-raising slogan since the invention of the wheel, but at St. Catherine's High School in Racine, Wisconsin, which is heavily in debt, it has had real meaning.

The school's 1,114 students and their teachers were challenged to find their individual ways of raising money to offset a $75,000 deficit. They reacted to the tune of $40,000 in six weeks, in some cases taking drastic action.

One sophomore with long hair had it sheared "butch-style" and collected a dollar each from eighty sponsors.

Father Mel Breit, a teacher, gave up smoking and collected forty-six dollars.

A girl collected fifteen dollars from her parents for staying home from a dance.

Father Leon J. Schneider, principal of St. Catherine's, went on a diet and got $128.85 for every pound he lost. Archbishop William E. Cousins of Milwaukee gave him five dollars a pound. Father Schneider dropped seventeen pounds to a svelte 193, for a total contribution of $2,275.45.

Nuns on the school's faculty raised about nine hundred dollars from two bake sales.

Thirteen girls earned eighty-five dollars by sewing

numerals on towels for Johnson's Wax, which has its home office in Racine. Other students took odd jobs.

A restaurant contributed seventy-five cents for each pizza sold on two nights and sold a total of 270 pizzas. Other merchants held "10 percent days," donating 10 percent of their profits to the school.

152. Plan Now to Boost Your Church Giving

Union Congregational Church in Green Bay, Wisconsin, aimed for a 50 percent increase in giving and pursued this goal with an all-out every-member canvass.

The plan, complete in how-to detail, was the product of years of experience of a veteran fund-raiser. The plan featured:

Step One

1. Positive budgeting, replacing "sharp pencil" methods.
2. Three potential budgets—essential, desirable, ideal (the sky was the limit).
3. Budget hearings by boards and committees and a general congregational meeting for in-depth discussions.
4. A standard of giving—one dollar per week for each one thousand dollars of annual income.
5. A realistic rating procedure for each family, concentrating on a family pledge to underwrite every program and service of the church.
6. A well-promoted fellowship dinner at a downtown hotel to inspire the entire congregation and to explain the reasons for giving money and time.
7. A high level of participation by members.
8. Face-to-face canvassing, emphasizing peer group contact.

Step Two

Members of the steering committee became leaders of the canvass teams which were grouped into echelons.

These steps were followed in training:

1. Presentation of plan, needs, and methods.
2. Individual commitment to family pledge before assignment to group for canvassing.
3. Selection of persons to canvass prospects whose giving rate was less than the canvasser's pledge.
4. The official calendar for all steps was capsuled into a workable but intense campaign period.

When the fellowship dinner was convened, 20 percent of the members had already pledged. Since the program first sought the highest-rated givers, much of the campaign goal was pledged before the official opening of the campaign.

By adopting the plan, financial leaders accepted the fact and responsibility that the pattern of giving would result in about 5 percent of the givers pledging 25 percent of the total goal.

153. Antiques

One thousand people attended an antique show and sale at First Parish Congregational Church in Wakefield, Massachusetts. The day-long sale netted one thousand five hundred dollars for the Protestant Youth Center at Baldwinsville. Thirty-six exhibitors from the New England area brought rare antiques to display and sell. Raymond Barlow of Windham, New Hampshire, an authority on Sandwich glass, displayed five hundred pieces of his collection. He also served as a "consultant" on antique glass brought to him by visitors to the show. Mr. Barlow has been conducting a campaign to make New England residents aware of the beauty and value of Sandwich glass. A similar type of show could be arranged on other communities where professionals exhibit their goods, with profits going toward a worthy project.

154. More Than Money

Stewardship is more than responsibility for *material* possessions such as money, real estate, and goods. You and I have a stewardship responsibility in all of life.

May our goal be to *improve* our stewardship in every area where we have control. Let us:

Improve our *stewardship of prayer* by an unhurried talk with God each day.

Improve our *stewardship of faith* by reading and studying the Bible each day.

Improve our *stewardship of time* by eliminating the trivial and concentrating on the important.

Improve our *stewardship of activities* by using them more effectively for God and our fellow men.

Improve our *stewardship of possessions* by setting aside at least 10 percent of our income and prayerfully dedicating it to the work of God's kingdom on earth.

Improve our *stewardship of life* by practicing the presence of God and living the teachings of Christ wherever we may be—always remembering our final accountability.

Worship

155. A Need for Changes in the Contemporary Church

With the four-day workweek becoming a reality, more churches should look into the possibility of moving away from their eleven o'clock Sunday worship syndrome. The practice is a carry-over from our churches' early rural background when the cows had to be milked and other chores done before families could go to church. Such is no longer the case, especially in our urban churches.

People today are aware of a deep spiritual hunger as reflected in religious music, drama, books, and interest in Eastern religions and astrology. They need something more meaningful than what is so frequently offered in the traditional service.

Here are some suggestions for making worship more meaningful in contemporary times:

1. Build people's inner resources by providing prayer groups and retreats.
2. There is a growing and painful loneliness among people so churches should do a better job of including these needs among their concerns.
3. Churches should show concern not only for youth but for the aged.
4. Strengthen your individual religious faith and trust in God through prayer, meditation, and reading.
5. Keep growing and learning. Continue your education through courses and reading.
6. Learn to trust people.
7. Accept the fact that the ministry is not only for the ordained.
8. Take seriously the ecumenical dimension and work together with people of other faiths to heal broken communities.
9. Build a sense of community among often-neglected single people.
10. Learn the techniques of good management so the church can be most effective.

156. Ecumenical Service Tears Down Walls

Littleton (Colorado) United Church of Christ engaged in an experimental service with several Roman Catholic parishes, dramatizing Matthew 5:21-26.

The worshipers were seated in five wedge-shaped sections facing the communion table. Each section represented a segment of society: the ghetto, the conservative establishment, youth, leaders of nations, and the liberals.

Paper walls had been erected to separate the five sections

of society. Conflict and anger were expressed, and shouts flew back and forth over the walls.

The climax of the service came in the invitation to the Lord's Supper. The following charge was given:

There is no more time to keep shouting at one another, for brotherhood will drown in the din. You cannot come to this altar to celebrate the life I gave you if you build barriers among yourselves. Look hard at yourself. The problem might not be someone else—it could be you. With determination you can destroy the old walls you have built.

The congregation then jerked down the walls and held hands across the aisles as they sang. Catholics and Protestants gave one another the bread and wine.

157. What Should Communicants Do During the Communion Service?

What should the worshipers do while the communion elements are being served? In some churches the organist plays softly, but a number of people find this distracting, especially when the music is inappropriate to the occasion. Silence has been tried, but the congregation begins to fidget.

A suggestion has been made that if this is a sharing service of a festival meal, then people should *speak* to one another. It is natural at a dinner party or a family meal to serve one another, not to merely pass things along. Individuals speak as various courses are in process.

At the Lord's Table the gathered communicants are servants of one another. That is why John describes the Last Supper in terms of footwashing. Therefore, those gathered for communion ought to serve the elements of communion to one another.

One of the reasons some groups do not go to the altar rail to be served by the clergyman is because they feel they should serve one another. The most symbolic way of doing this is to speak as the bread and wine are passed. Short, expressive phrases that can be used are "Peace be with you" or "The Lord be with you" or "Receive Christ" or "Do this in remembrance of him." In each case, the answer "Amen" can be given. Such communication is appropriate to the communion service.

158. Church-Schoolers Take Leadership in Worship Services

In an effort to communicate to parents in the congregation about what is going on at various age levels in the Edina-Morningside Church in Edina, Minnesota, a new approach was used.

Instead of listening to a children's sermon by the minister on the second Sunday of each month (traditionally family Sunday), each church school department took the responsibility for part of the service once during the year. The teachers and children shared briefly with the congregation something that evolved in their classroom sessions. This included summaries given by members of different classes about a particular unit of study, a prayer, or a litany. Other classes showed group drawings, projects, or relevant art work or gave a musical program.

With the help of their teachers, the young people decided what their part in the worship service would be.

159. Worship and Education Combined

The Oak Park (Illinois) First Congregational Church combines Sunday worship and Christian education into one period, with worship at 10:00 A.M. and seminars at 11:00. Four series of seminars of up to six sessions begin in September. After three months, a free Sunday with an all-congregational program takes place during the eleven o'clock hour.

Seminar subjects include housing, parks, mental health, drugs, generation gap problems, the Apochrypha, New and Old Testament studies, community organizations, and interpersonal relationships. A brochure, distributed in advance to the congregation, describes the various courses.

160. Favorite Hymns in Centennial Album

When St. John Church in Wyandotte, Michigan, observed its one hundreth anniversary, the congregation wanted a remembrance of the occasion. So a record was made of the congregation's favorite hymns and anthems. During the regular worship hour certain numbers were recorded while others were done at special occasions.

161. Put Your Pastor's Sermon to Work

What happens to sermons preached in church each week? Most go into the "barrel" to be used in the minister's next pastorate or to be completely forgotten. Some need to be quietly buried; others need to be put to work. Here's a method that can put them to work:

1. The minister should write his sermons or tape them.
2. The complete sermon should be edited and then mimeographed for mailing to the sick, shut-ins, nonresident members, and others on the mailing list of the church.
3. A small supply of sermons should be kept in the vestibule.
4. Especially well-received messages might be properly typed and submitted to magazines specializing in homiletics.

5. A questionnaire in the Sunday bulletin with five to eight questions on the sermon helps to maintain careful attention and to create a demand for printed copy.

6. Short, pointed passages from the sermon should be used in bulletins or newsletters. A standard heading, such as "The pastor says . . ." will encourage reading.

7. Use the mimeographed sermons as a basis for discussion in small groups.

8. Make a list of the sermons preached during the year, present it to your congregation via a printed medium and ask which one they would like to have repeated.

9. Make a file with such topics as loneliness, fear, stewardship, faith, prayer, etc., and place sermons in folders for use as reference. These will be used by people in distress, students, and individuals needing material for worship programs.

162. Five Questions to Help You Evaluate Worship in Your Church

1. What do you expect in group worship? Realize that learning to worship, like learning to swim, requires interest, effort, and discipline.

2. What is reverence? Does it involve joy and/or sobriety? which is your primary focus? Remember Christians have received the *Good* News—and should look redeemed.

3. Where should we revere God? Is the sanctuary itself holy?

4. Is your sanctuary safe for diversity? Is there tolerance of style and choice of worship for all persons?

5. Are worshipers spectators? Or is worship a process in which all have an opportunity to plan and participate?

163. Five Ideas to Help You Improve Your Worship Program

1. Let all worshipers participate in preparing for services. Use forms on which everyone can write about his most joyous experience of the week.
2. Include an elective course for adults on worship and religious music—classical, jazz, gospel—in the church school, on a retreat.
3. Develop a worship committee composed of lay members and community people—artists, musicians, young people.
4. Try a worship festival. Invite resource persons, display banners and photographs, experiment, be ecumenical.
5. Make learning to worship a year-long priority of your church, and build participation among *all* age groups.

164. New Forms of Celebration Emerging

Changes are taking place in the worship services of our churches. No congregation is too small or too large for new forms of worship to be utilized. Here are some suggestions:

1. The utilization of banners, art, color, and other non-verbal forms of communication.
2. The use of contemporary music, folk masses, youthful rock in good taste, contemporary congregational singing.
3. Think of worship as joy and celebration. People will begin to "enjoy" worship.
4. Moments of mission, which are readings from contemporary literature in today's language, will help a staid worship service. Readings from modern translations of the Bible make for more attentive congregations.
5. Informality helps to make worship warm and friendly. A

time of greetings, when everyone greets his neighbor, is one step toward informality. Clapping during a hymn is another. Some congregations have moved out the pews. The dress of the minister and people is more informal.

6. Sensation of touch is being tried. Most people are used to a handshake in public, but the expression of genuine Christian love can have meaning in an embrace, holding hands, arms entwined in a friendship circle, or a "holy kiss."

7. The minister is looked on not so much as an authoritative figure imparting the Word but as an enabler who shares in a dialogue, provides opportunity for feedback, and encourages the sharing of ideas.

8. Joys and concerns can be announced by members of the worshiping congregation. There may be prayer, discussion, and talking about what is in the hearts of people.

9. The Lord's Supper is taking on new forms. The elements can be taken in a variety of ways, some quite informal. The proper spirit will help people to share worshipfully in the new forms.

Youth

165. Summer Fun Goes All Year

When the 1970 summer fun program, sponsored by St. John United Church of Christ, ended its season of cultural enrichment for children in the deprived area of St. Charles, Missouri, the teen-age group leaders asked, "Where do we sign up to help again next year?"

More than eighty children were enrolled, participating in song fests, dancing, drama, story time, arts, and crafts. Resource persons, including a Navajo Indian who demonstrated and taught sign language and the skills of beadcraft and a folk singer, were invited to participate. A student priest, a student from a theological seminary, seven adults and ten teenagers from the church assisted in directing the program.

Volunteers from St. John Church prepared and served lunch daily with the YMCA cosponsoring the eight-week program. Finance came from the U.S. Department of Agriculture's food and nutrition service.

Three get-togethers with the children during subsequent school year vacations were arranged. The project emerged as a going concern in which persons of various ages and races enjoyed one another's company in an atmosphere of mutual acceptance and growth.

166. Junior High Church Program Has Drawing Power

"We had our problems. Boy! Did we have our problems! Our confirmation program was a struggle. Our junior high fellowship had precious few members, our youth choir had collapsed, and our board of Christian education was hammering for a proposal that would appeal to the youth of the church in an era when church does not appeal to youth." Such a lament could have come from any number of ministers.

At St. Paul United Church of Christ in Chelsea, Michigan, a program has been prepared that has brought some exciting changes for a Saturday procedure.

At 9 A.M. the pastor takes the eighth grade confirmation class for one hour. The youth director has the seventh graders. Class sessions deal with world religions, God, Christ, church, and the person. There are field trips and audiovisual programs.

At 10 A.M. comes a "Coke" break followed at 10:15 by a forty-five-minute musical training session led by the choir director or organist.

From 11 A.M. to noon, recreation time in the game room

takes precedence. Along with competition and games of skill, service projects are planned and undertaken.

Two mothers serve lunch for seventy-five cents per person. New friendships are promoted around the table. At 12:30 P.M. everyone is dismissed.

The new program has been extremely effective. Over 90 percent of the eligible junior high students have been regularly in attendance, and the program for this age group is moving forward.

Other facets of the program are a phone-alert system for meetings, program-planning units, mothers' schedule for special assignments, staff sessions, parents' orientation, potluck suppers, and much more.

167. Summer Hostel for Youth

Each summer the educational building of Rosedale United Church in Montreal, Quebec, is converted into a hostel to accommodate organized youth groups desiring to visit Montreal. Many churches in America study the cultural composition of Montreal, so the church provides inexpensive accommodations for church groups, high school and college young people, and YMCA and YWCA groups.

This is the only hostel in Montreal that caters especially to youth. It seeks to foster fellowship and understanding among people of different nationalities, races, and religions.

The hostel operates from the first of June to mid-September. Eighty persons can be accommodated in eight dormitories. Guests bring their own sleeping bags, other bedding, and towels. The rate is $2.25, including breakfast. Limited use of a kitchen is available, and showers and washrooms are plentiful.

With America traveling, many churches could open their doors to the wayfarers.

168. Seniors High with a Purpose

United Souls of America (USA) is the name of a high school group that meets at Ridgeview Church in White Plains, New York, on Saturdays from 4 to 6:30 P.M. USA was selected because it suggests that the group is a union of diverse people working together for common purposes. "Soul" is the key word in the name because it suggests a bond between people that transcends ethnic, racial, and religious divisions.

The USA participates in the worship services, and proceeds from fund-raising activities have gone toward buying a gift for the church. One meeting at the pastor's home emphasized a dimension in sharing. Each participant was asked to bring an object to the meeting which represented a meaningful event, occasion, or person in his or her experience. Objects shared were photographs, books, gifts, handcrafts, a "Linus blanket," etc.

169. Setting Up a Drug Prevention Center

What should a drug prevention center and hotline offer? The Melodyland Center in Anaheim, California, offers:
1. Phone counseling. A twenty-four hour hotline deals with drugs, suicide, pregnancies, loneliness, and many other problems. Concerned and experienced counselors utilizing the most recent and reliable referrals in the area are available on four public lines.
2. Hotline hours. Folk-rock music and well-known youth speakers are featured every Tuesday evening at Melody-

land in entertainment relating to the encouragement and guidance of young people.

3. Hospital and prison visitation. A vital outreach of musical programs and personal visitation to hospitals, rest homes, mental institutions, jails, and children's homes is carried on.

4. Pregnancy and abortion counseling. A special effort is made to assist unwed mothers-to-be in choosing a course of action.

5. Youth paper. *Trinity Times* is a monthly publication with a positive approach to youth problems.

6. Employment. A free placement service for all ages. It seeks part- or full-time employment and a reliable source of promising personnel for employers is made available.

7. Personal problem counseling. Informal counseling by appointment is available to discuss such problem areas as drug abuse; marital, premarital, and interpersonal relationships; spiritual, emotional, and financial situations.

8. Speakers bureau. Former drug users and drug prevention and rehabilitation administrators are on call for drug program consultation with interested organizations.

9. Music. A musical group, A SALT (Always Sharing a Living Truth) represents musical groups ranging in size from one to fifty and in styles from country to contemporary. These groups have performed in schools, service clubs, churches, hospitals, coffeehouses, correctional institutions, and many other organizations.

170. A Home for Runaways

First Congregational Church in Forth Worth, Texas, sparked the purchase of a large two-story house, which had previously been converted into four apartments, as a shelter for runaways and young people who have nowhere else to go.

The shelter is open twenty-four hours a day. Food, laundry, transportation, and other daily needs of the twenty or so residents, are funded by a grant from the Texas Criminal Justice Council and the Tarrant County Commissioners, who made the statement that "the basic business of the county is not streets and sewers, but people and their needs."

Fairmont Station, as the facility is known, provides shelter, food, basic counseling, and referral services to the 110 persons who find their way there each month. Volunteers from First Church have become involved in the ministry to runaways.

171. Musical Teenagers

A group of from four to six teenagers who have combined their talents in singing and guitar accompaniment is called on every Sunday, as well as through the week, to participate in the church program of Immanuel United Church of Christ in Dalton, Illinois. The young people take part in worship services and in the church school where they offer a monthly hymn sing; they perform at wedding services and at receptions. Both youth and adults have found the music to be a meaningful service.

172. Clap Your Hands

A standing ovation for youth? That is the response given to the high school young people at Second Congregational Church in Rockford, Illinois. The youth presented a musical gospel with songs and messages in the modern folk mode. There were strings and percussion instruments, along with piano accompaniments. Twenty singers helped with the service. The young people received a standing ovation from the congregation, which overflowed from the sanctuary into the street.

173. Youth Group Discusses
Sermon in Sunday Service

First Congregational Church in Kalamazoo, Michigan, has developed a successful worship enrichment program for senior high young people. It began in response to criticism by youth that worship services were irrelevant or worse. Young people wanted the opportunity to ask questions, to disagree with what was being said, to clap when they liked the music, and to worship God in a less structured and formal service.

So First Church provides an alternative. The pastor's sermons are mimeographed and handed out before worship. Each Sunday a leader gathers the students in the church parlor, and, while the service is being held, they discuss the sermon in a no-holds-barred session.

When specialized areas of Christian concern are introduced in the sermons, persons with expertise are invited to join the group. A psychiatrist might be invited to sit in with the youth when anxiety is the topic. A black person from the community or member of another minority would join the group if the topic were race relations.

The only provision is that the youth must agree either to attend the regular service or the parlor group. They are discouraged from coming to church just to hang around because of parents' wishes or to see friends.

The Christian education committee feels that this model has been very successful and would work anywhere. Sermon texts should be prepared in advance and a suitable teacher enlisted.

174. A New Twist at Summer Day Camp— Black Culture

Harambee is Swahili for "build together." And building together has been a major experience of the children at the Plymouth Settlement House in Louisville, Kentucky.

The children took part in a summer program modeled on the organization of an African village—with a chief, tribes, and warriors. This model was devised as a means of acquainting black children with their history. "Our purpose," said the executive director, Morris F. X. Jeff, Jr., "was to help the children see Africa in a different light than in the negative Hollywood version."

During the two camping periods (the first session was for seven-to eleven-year-olds and the second, twelve to fourteen) the children learned that in Africa the land was communal, the family was the core of the society, social life was well organized. The village cultural heritage and the political institutions, including army, courts, and economic structures, were also studied.

The camp placed much emphasis on role-playing and dramatics to teach the tools that are necessary to make it in our society. Songs, symbols, art forms, poems, folk dancing, and folktales were also included.

Personal Notes on
Helpful Programs